PILL BOXES
on the Western Front

PILL BOXES
on the Western Front

A Guide to the Design, Construction and Use of Concrete Pill Boxes 1914-1918

Peter Oldham

LEO COOPER
LONDON

First published in Great Britain in 1995 by Leo Cooper,
190 Shaftesbury Avenue, London WC2H 8JL,
an imprint of Pen & Sword Books Limited,
47 Church Street, Barnsley, South Yorkshire S70 2AS

*For up-to-date information on other titles produced under
the Leo Cooper imprint, please telephone or write to:*

Pen & Sword Books Ltd
FREEPOST
47 Church Street
Barnsley
South Yorkshire
S70 2BR
Telephone (24 hours): 01226 734555

ISBN 0-85052-418-0

British Library Cataloguing in Publication Data

Designed and produced by Wharncliffe Publishing Limited (Book Division)

Printed by Redwood Books Ltd
Trowbridge, Wiltshire

CONTENTS

INTRODUCTION

During several visits to the battlefields of the Ypres Salient and the Somme in the 1980s I came across a number of concrete edifices, often in the middle of a field and frequently showing signs of severe damage from shell fire. In many instances the remaining concrete structures were the only visible evidence that anything at all remarkable had happened in the immediate vicinity. Having spent some time working in the production and supply of aggregates and concrete in the construction industry, I had a good understanding of the logistical problems of producing such constructions. I was filled with curiosity as to how the builders had managed to transport cement and aggregates in wet, nightmarish conditions, erect wooden formwork and steel reinforcements, and mix and place concrete — all when somebody 100 yards away was trying to kill them, and when to make a noise or show light at night would cause a hail of bombs and bullets.

It was also apparent that, despite the conditions during construction, the structures were on the whole extremely durable and well built. Images of cement slopped around a château gate were soon dispelled. Properly engineered steel and dense concrete produced structures which, apart from being generally shell-proof, were also in many ways better than the structural and civil engineering projects I saw being constructed in the 1970s and 1980s. The concrete bunkers, pill boxes and observation posts still remaining on the Western Front have a much longer potential life than more recently built tower blocks and motorway bridges, unless they are deliberately removed to make way for something else.

I remember standing in a field beside a small British pill box just outside Hébuterne on the Somme battlefield, facing Gommecourt Park in what was the British front line, trying to imagine the scene on the morning of 1 July, 1916, when the 56th Division left its trench-line here and walked towards the trees about 200 yards away. Why wasn't the pill box mentioned in any reports? It must have played a major role in the action. And how was it possible to build such a structure right on the front line anyway? In trying to answer such questions, a search of contemporary and modern books failed to produce any information. Only after several years of delving into records at the Public Records Office, the Imperial War Museum, the Royal Engineers Corps Library and those of divers other organizations was my problem solved. With a slight tinge of disappointment I discovered that the pill box in question did not figure in the July 1916 attack as it was built during June 1918 in what was then a reserve line — the enemy being about half a mile away.

This book is therefore a result of the lack of available information, and what I considered to be a need to research, investigate and compile the numerous recorded plans, drawings, maps and reports held by the Public Records Office, the Imperial War Museum and the Royal Engineers Corps Library. I have combined these records with information gleaned from regimental records and divisional and unit histories, and pieces kindly supplied by friends in both Britain and Europe who are also interested in the traumatic events of 1914-1918.

Whilst the book is intended to provide information on the design, development and construction of concrete pill boxes and bunkers, I have not attempted to discuss their tactical or strategic use other than in some description of their capture. There are many who are more knowledgeable on these aspects and could do a far better job than I. But I hope to inspire any visitor to the Western Front — or any armchair visitor or reader on the subject — to consider the problems of those who constructed the monoliths, and appreciate why and how they were built. My interest on strong defensive positions also stems from man's natural instinct in times of trouble to search for a safe haven in which to shelter rather than brave the storm.

I have not attempted to define or explain the term 'pill box'. Having read and listened to several ideas and theories on its origin, I have concluded that, as with any description which has evolved rather than been invented, to refer to its coining is most probably misleading. The common explanation, that it derives from its similarity to a box which dispenses nasty things like tablets, is less than convincing. It is worth noting that only a small percentage of concrete constructions built by both sides during the First World War can be termed pill boxes – having one or more embrasures to allow the use of a machine-gun. The vast majority were built for shelter from shells and mortars. Along with observation posts, command and communication centres, heavy gun emplacements, field hospitals and kitchens, they were vital in conditions of static warfare.

The term 'pill box' first appeared in print in *The Times* on 2 August, 1917, and soon became a generic name for any concrete shelter. Early official British usage tended towards 'pill box' rather than 'pill-box' or 'pillbox', so I have used the original style in this book. Similarly, 'dug out', 'machine-gun', 'shell fire' and 'loop hole' – all words which existed before the First World War – appear in various official and contemporary records as hyphenated, unhyphenated, one word and two words. In the main text of this book I have attempted to be consistent.

The spelling of many Flemish place names has changed, and names were in any case spelled differently by British, French, German and Belgian personnel at the time. I have used the old spelling (which varies according to the nationality of the writer) in original source material and the modern spelling in the main text to keep words in context – the differences are minor, and the reader should have no difficulty in identifying places and key geographical points.

ACKNOWLEDGEMENTS

I am indebted to the following persons and organizations for the help and assistance given in the form of advice, information, photographs and books loaned, tea and sympathy.

Dick Knights and Jock Hamilton-Baillie; Mike Willis and other staff at the Imperial War Museum; Tony and Teddy Noyes; Aleks Deseyne and the Zonnebeke Streeksmuseum; Simon Jones of the Royal Engineers Museum at Chatham, and the Corps Library staff; Phillipe Delameillure of Menin and Pierre Capelle of Trescault; Tony de Bruyne of the Herinnerings Museum, Ypres; Captain Smith and the curator of the Royal Monmouthshire Royal Engineers Museum, Monmouth, and numerous infantry regiments and units who have been very helpful in providing information; and last but not least, Jennifer for untold patience and understanding.

CHAPTER ONE

Development

It did not take man long to discover that stones when stuck together were stronger and more stable than loosely laid stones. Both Egyptians and Greeks made use of mortar, whilst the Romans, who inherited the knowledge, developed and adapted materials to improve their performance. They found that by adding volcanic earth, pozzolana, or finely-ground tiles, to burnt lime and sand they could produce a stronger mortar with superior qualities. Defence works like Hadrian's Wall could be strengthened by infilling with concrete. Walls, villas and farms, as well as public buildings and castles, could be made safe and strong.

With the departure of the Romans from Britain, the art of concrete making was forgotten. The Saxons blended local limestone with burnt lime in about 700 AD, although it was the Normans who made full use of lime mortars to infill and strengthen the stone walls of their castles.

The first full technical assessment of cements was made by John Smeaton, a Yorkshire engineer, to determine the best material to build the Eddystone Lighthouse off Plymouth in 1758. Following this, several proprietary cements were produced in England, such as the Reverend James Parker's Roman Cement and James Frost's Frost's Cement, using a process developed by Vicat in France.

The first 'proper' or Portland cement was made by Joseph Aspdin in Wakefield in the 1820s, and named after its similarity to Portland building stone. Joseph's younger son, William, took the idea south and opened a cement works at Rotherhithe on the Thames estuary. Joseph meanwhile opened works in Gateshead on Tyneside, and in Germany. His business was later taken over, and the cement product improved, by Isaac Johnson.

Much early use of concrete was for domestic building and civil engineering. Military engineers seem not to have been impressed, and between the 1830s and 1870s gave preference to traditional fortification materials like stone and brick. Following the construction of Newhaven Fort in 1865 interest in the use of concrete by military engineers increased, but this was too late for the rush of fort building prompted by the perceived threat of invasion by France.

After trials at Shoeburyness in 1877, concrete was judged to be superior to stone in resisting explosive shells, although the political situation at the time necessitated only the updating of existing forts and some harbour defence works. Large fortress building was left to those on mainland Europe.

By the end of the 19th century fortification design had become a highly technical form of engineering. Forts throughout Europe were built, modernized, refortified and strengthened to keep ahead of the basic equation: the strength of masonry versus the power of explosive.

The geometrical design of French forts had been perfected by Vauban in the latter part of the 17th century, and the later development of breech-loading guns, followed by the more important advent of barrel-rifling, called for new thought in defensive engineering. Belgium's forts were modernized by Henri Brialmont, with Antwerp defended by an impregnable ring of eleven forts surrounding the inner sanctum.

After the 1870 Franco-Prussian war the defences of France were closely examined. General de Rivières suggested and designed massive, solid fortifications able to withstand repeated bombardment. The use of cast-chilled armour with its ability to resist high-velocity projectiles, coupled with concrete for bedding and a firm foundation, produced a solidity beyond the dreams of earlier engineers. To redress the balance, high explosive picric acid, trinitro-phenol, was developed by the Germans, and followed shortly by the French equivalent, melinite.

At the opening of the 20th century Germany kept a defensive and watchful eye on France, who, like Belgium, had steadily maintained her defences. The twitching and rattling of sabres caused both sides to look closely at defences. On the eastern side of the border forts were built with concrete and steel in mutually protective positions, while on the western side similar work was in hand. The French developed the concept of an outer skin, or burster layer, of high-quality concrete over a shock-absorbing layer of loose sand or earth. The inner layer of concrete would withstand any residual shock, so the central core, and the inhabitants, would be unaffected. The Belgians had also been busy modernizing their Brialmont forts, although the same science and attention to detail was not utilized.

The largest artillery pieces of the time, 42cm howitzers (christened Big Berthas), were used in August, 1914, against the stalwart defenders of the Liège and other Belgian forts. Earlier calculations were found to be inadequate when confronted with such armaments technology — the forts had been designed to withstand the rigours of earlier warfare. German engineers, examining the wreckage of those at Antwerp, Namur and Maubeuge, were surprised to find concrete-work much weaker than expected. Unscrupulous building contractors, shortages of cement and inoperable labour laws were reported as the causes.

After the First World War the French investigated the performances of the Belgian forts, which had crumbled easily, and those at Verdun in France of the same approximate age which had withstood much greater bombardments without suffering the same fate.[1] They paid considerable attention to the design and construction of those which had been modernized between 1890 and 1912. The original masonry, one and a half metres thick, had a covering of two layers of reinforced concrete with a bed of sand between to absorb the shock of shells detonated by the upper layer. The total thickness was six metres and the quality of concrete was high, having been vigorously tested and approved by the Laboratoire de Boulogne. Each cubic metre of concrete contained 400 kilograms of cement (used today for highly stressed motorway bridge beams and pre-stressed high-rise buildings).

The Belgian forts at Liège and Namur had been constructed and modernized with less attention to quality. Civilian contractors strengthened the existing one and three-quarter to two and a half metres of masonry with an inner skin of unreinforced concrete with a cement content of between 175 and 250 kilograms per cubic metre (used today as light foundations for single-storey buildings or houses). As a result their forts, although stoutly defended, did not withstand the bombardment of the German

Fort Loncin, Liège, shortly after it was captured by the Germans in 1914 (top) and today (bottom), a tomb for soldiers killed during the bombardment when a heavy howitzer shell exploded the magazine. Poor quality concrete used in the constructions resulted in severe damage and the complete collapse of the gun cupola.

42cm howitzers. Early attacks on those around Liège using field artillery failed to smash them, so heavy siege guns were brought up. Pontisse Fort fell first, followed by those at Embourg, Liers, Fléron, Boncelles, Lantin, Chaudfontaine and finally Loncin, where the concrete failed to withstand penetration by shells and the magazine exploded.

1 *Les Fortifications Permanentes Pendant la Guerre* by General Benoit (Paris 1921).

CHAPTER TWO

Solid Defences

The Germans, having smashed the Belgian forts, pressed on with their Schlieffen Plan — which demanded much mobility of both materials and men. Before long the French, Belgian and British armies had prevented their progress, and both sides dug in along a line stretching from Nieuport on the Belgian coast to Pfetterhouse on the Swiss border. In early 1915 both sides tried advancing, but defence proved easier and less costly. The result was stalemate.

Trenches on both sides were made more solid, more complicated and more permanent, but especially on the German side. British intelligence were aware of the superior strengths of these enemy trenches, which would cause them no surprise had their network been monitoring the foreign press. In its morning edition of 20 October, 1915, the Dutch newspaper *Der Telegraaf* reported that two Rhine barges, the *Vereinigte Spediteur* and the *Schiffer zur Heereslieferung*, manned by military crews, were bringing 20,000 tonnes of basalt and gravel from Germany through The Netherlands for concrete works on the Western Front. This was considered by Sir Edward Grey, the British Foreign Secretary, as a direct contravention of the Hague Convention of 1907, which prohibited the passage of military supplies through a neutral state. Diplomatic complaints were made to the Dutch government accordingly. It was also reported that many of these 'certified' loads concealed guns and ammunition.

While the Dutch expounded denials and excuses, the number of barges making passage through The Netherlands escalated. By the end of March, 1916, over sixty barges, each carrying up to 2,000 tonnes of gravel, sand and cement, had been off-loaded in Belgian towns on the River Lys, such as Menin and Courtrai. By September the number had risen to 300 barges, and the Dutch were well satisfied by supporting German certificates which assured them the concrete-making materials were to be used for civilian purposes only. Herr Schlubach, a specialist sent to The Hague by the German government, persuaded them to increase the allowable tonnage from 75,000 to 420,000 tonnes.

However, the British ambassador to The Hague, Sir Alan Johnstone, succeeded in prompting the Dutch to investigate the use to which these materials were being put. In September, 1916, with the consent of the Imperial German government, two Dutch army engineers visited occupied territory in Belgium and northern France. Because of the 'dangerous situation' near the front, inspection was confined to the rear zones.

The Dutch were more than pleased to report that the materials were indeed for civilian use. When the Belgians had fallen back before the Germans in the early months of the war, they had wantonly destroyed roads, bridges and railway lines. The caring Germans, full of good will and friendliness, were shipping in materials to repair the damage. Over 300 kilometres of pavé road had been macadamized, using four tonnes of road metal per metre length; 2,368 kilometres had been repaired; the banks of the River Scheldt had been strengthened following bad weather and the port of Ghent had been extended (for civilian purposes, naturally). These works used all the materials brought through The Netherlands, plus stone extracted from existing Belgian quarries, leaving no surplus for military uses at the front. The Dutch authorities were well satisfied with the pacific nature of the works for which the materials were used.

The British were not amused, especially when the same barges that brought the materials in were used on their return to Germany

Some bunkers were built in the front line. This German one, in front of Wieltje, was only 150 yards from the British front line.

to carry other materials — broken guns, rifles, shell-cases, military scrap, requisitioned metals and metallic ore.

Relations between London and The Hague worsened. The enemy were using rolling-stock for transporting men and armaments, and the Dutch eased the demand on this stock by allowing the passage of barges filled with materials for constructing fortifications. British Admiralty Intelligence in July, 1917, reported:

> ...had we forced Holland to discontinue this traffic through her waterways the Hindenburg defences could have never been built, except at enormous sacrifice of other necessary operations.

Meanwhile, Belgian escapees reported pre-cast works producing concrete-block forts south of Antwerp and at Burcht and Hoboken.

The British army had been busy during this diplomatic wrangling. Vimy Ridge fell, and the concrete defences were examined from a military engineering aspect to assess the origin of the aggregates used. Samples were examined by the Geological Society in London, which concluded that many of the stones present pink muscovite, biotite granite, pink rhyolite, types of felsite and andesite lava, gneiss with hornblende and epidote — were foreign to Belgium and northern France and were known to come from quarries east of the Rhine. This was confirmed by Commandant Stevens, a geologist of the Belgian mission.

After the Messines and Ypres battles of 1917, a specialist committee was formed to identify the source of the aggregates used by the Germans. The committee included, among others, A. Straham of the Geological Survey of Great Britain; Xavier Stainier, Professor of Geology at the University of Ghent, Belgium; Major Edgeworth David of the Australian army, Professor of Geology at the University of Sydney, Australia; Sir J. J. H. Teall, Director of the Geological Survey of Great Britain; Dr A. Harker, President of the Geological Society and Lecturer on Petrology at the University of Cambridge.

Concrete and aggregate samples from the ridges and other locations around Ypres were examined and found to be of teutonic origin. German quarries at Linz, Erpel, Bassenheim and Niedermending were identified as sources of the stones, as were

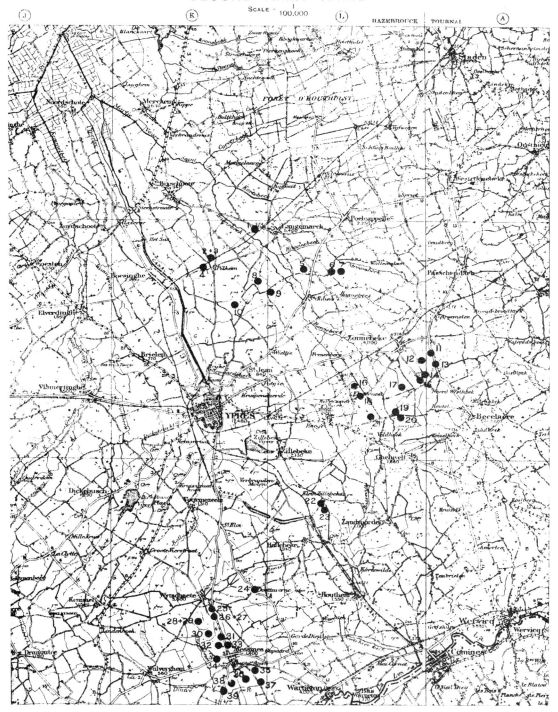

Samples taken of German concrete and aggregates from pill boxes and bunkers at Messines and the Ypres Salient were sent to England for examination by geological experts. The aggregates proved to come from German sources; in allowing their passage, the Dutch authorities had broken the 1907 Hague Convention. This was denied by the Dutch government.

river gravels from around Ziegelhausen and Freiburg. These findings were reported to the Dutch, but by then it was too late — they had earned more than enough Deutschmarks.

Others were also profiting from the supply of concrete materials to the Germans. The British Associated Portland Cement Company enjoyed a healthy trade with The Netherlands, which was halted by the British government following a report that English cement bags and seals marked 'A.P.C.' had been found in captured German trenches. It was claimed that the company was selling cement to the Dutch, who sold it on to the Germans. Strong denials were forthcoming: the Antwerp Portland Cement (then in German hands) was said to be the real culprit. It supplied inferior cement in 'A.P.C.' bags with lead seals before the war and, as Associated Portland Cement did not use lead seals, the bags and seals found were Belgian, not British. Besides, the ban on sales to the Dutch was affecting profits. The ban was lifted.

It was later reported by an English prisoner captured by the Germans that English cement bags were seen in the back areas. Such news was not unique and the scandal became more widespread:

> Yet another piece of news which disgusted us was the incredible action of our government in selling huge quantities of cement to the Dutch, knowing that this was to be passed to the Germans for the construction of the much vaunted Hindenburg Line.[2]

In addition to German materials shipped to Belgium and France, some were purchased directly from the Dutch, permitted under the Hague Convention. By transporting Dutch gravel into Belgium via Hansweert, and sand via Sas van Gent, the Germans were able to augment their supplies in September, 1917, by about 40,000 tones of aggregate and 2,100 tonnes of cement. They were also sourcing large quantities locally. Several Belgian and French cement works were in German hands, the Antwerp Portland Cement works and the Obourg works near Mons in Belgium being just two of many. In Belgium and France quarries and sand-pits were commandeered, offering the benefits of materials produced close to the point of use and minimizing labour, transport and costs. To exploit this, teams of geologists, *Geologen Stelle*, were attached to German forces to investigate and advise on where materials could be extracted, available quantities, and the best way of working them. Working in an advisory capacity, leaving the quarrying and supervision to the corps or divisions, a typical geological attachment was:

Corps	Landaufnahme
Field survey company	Research geologists
Professional geologist	Geological leader
Assistant geologist	Geological group
Draughtsman	Draughtsmen
Clerk	Clerks
Boring party of	
four or five men	

As well as advising on aggregates for concrete and roads, the *Geologen Stelle* advised on the construction and siting of trenches, where dug-outs could be excavated and how subterranean water and wet ground could be avoided. Such information was essential for planning defences such as the Hindenburg Line. Yet the Hindenburg Line and the German withdrawal of March, 1917, seem to have taken British intelligence completely by surprise.

The British army made do without a geological advisory unit for most of the war, relying on Royal Engineers officers with some (generally limited) understanding of geology. A proposal was tabled in September, 1918, to establish geological advisory units at General Headquarters and each of the armies in the field, comprising:

At General Headquarters
Commandant (Geologist) Major or Lieutenant-Colonel
Assistant Commandant (Geologist) Captain
Clerk/typist one
Draughtsmen three

At each Army Headquarters
Geologist Captain or Lieutenant
Clerk/typist one
Draughtsman one
Although the proposal was agreed, the plan was put forward too late to materialize.

The American army were quicker off the mark and appointed Lieutenant-Colonel Brooks as geologist to the American armies in 1917. He was later given an assistant, and it was eventually

In 1916 the Germans facing Ypres constructed reinforced concrete pill boxes and bunkers, such as this one near Zonnebeke. Large tonnages of concrete materials — gravel, sand, cement and steel — were required.

agreed that a total of seventeen geologists would be employed to handle the work, although not all were appointed before hostilities ceased.

During 1915, and into 1916, the Germans were finding concrete, especially when reinforced with steel, a very useful material in ground conditions which did not allow the digging of deep dug-outs. Around the Ypres Salient, for example, ground water posed a problem and it was easier to build up than to build down. Here the Germans constructed many bunkers, blockhouses and machine-gun emplacements, *Mannschafts Eisenbeton Understände*, or MEBUs, (soon to be named pill boxes by the British troops). Pre-war military field-engineering manuals, such as that by Brunner,[3] were updated following experience gained in the field. *Cover from Shell Fire*,[4] advising on wood and earth protective dug-outs, recommended that the best protecting course was concrete, especially when reinforced with steel. By this time the use of railway rails and heavy iron bars placed close together had been found to separate the concrete into layers, thereby weakening the structure. Smaller, well-spaced rods proved more effective.

The British policy of being permanently on the offensive did not permit the official adoption of heavy concrete structures. The general staff, based well behind the lines at Montreuil, considered that good shelter from shell fire would sap the morale of troops, who were better off in their wet trenches. If British troops must have the luxury of strong concrete blockhouses, then let them take them from the Germans.

However, the protection of artillery observers was considered important, and it was soon discovered that clay roof-tiles did not provide much protection from anything more serious than heavy rain. Roofs of houses and barns selected for observation posts in

Many bunkers and pill boxes were built into damaged buildings for concealment. This one constructed near Becelaere in 1916 used the ruins of a farmhouse.

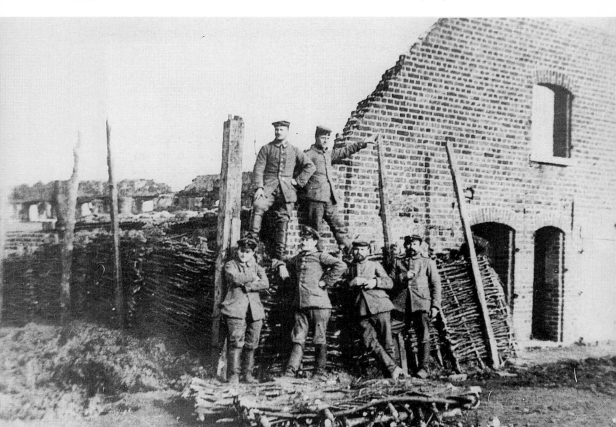

strategic places were strengthened, either by constructing a reinforced concrete tower up through the roof, or simply filling the whole roof space with concrete. Foundations and ground-floor walls then had to be strengthened to take the extra weight and any shock from a direct hit.

In April, 1916, the Royal Monmouthshire Royal Engineers constructed a Royal Artillery observation post in a house in the village of Potijze, north-east of Ypres. The 30-foot high tower, named Red Tile House or RAOP No.11, allowed observation well beyond the German lines. It received a direct hit not long after construction, becoming the first known instance of such a structure withstanding a 5.9″ shell. The design was then circulated, with variations, and ten others were constructed in the same vicinity during the following months. Hussar Farm and Hasler House observation posts, constructed in July, 1916, are good examples.

Production of an observation tower for the artillery presented the Royal Engineers with a number of problems, such as obtaining and transporting forward supplies of suitable materials. Brick rubble and hard core were easily available, but were known to produce soft concrete. Harder stone or gravel with sand and cement was required. Large supplies of broken stone and ballast had been in demand by the British army since early in the war to repair pavé roads and tracks, which suffered from traffic a great deal heavier and more concentrated than that for which they had been built.

Landowners and quarry operators jumped at the chance to profit from such a needy customer as the British army. Limestone hills at Marquise between Calais and Boulogne had long been a quarrying area, supplying local steelworks, such as those at Outreau in Boulogne, as well as the construction industry all over northern France. The price of stone varied with the quality: one of the larger quarries, at Beaulieu, operated by Raymond, Galtier et Brizard, rated between four and five francs per tonne, while the slightly harder stone from Lonquety quarry, near Beaulieu, fetched up to 6.50 francs per tonne in February, 1916. Demand was high and the price was geared accordingly in August, 1915, the Vallée Heureuse quarry increased its price from five to 5.50 francs per tonne.

Red House observation station was built to give the Royal Artillery means to direct fire accurately. The ability to withstand a direct hit from a heavy shell (5.9″) was a major advantage. The house was rebuilt after the war around the concrete tower, and demolished about 1970.

*German prisoners working in the quarries at Marquise, near Boulogne. Several
limestone quarries were operated by the Royal Engineers, using German labour,
once it was found to be cheaper than purchasing stone from civilian suppliers.*
(Imperial War Museum, Q 9702)

River gravel and sand was preferred for concrete, and supplies
were obtained from a number of small pits. Drouard Frères et
Cie at Incheville supplied flint gravel at 2.70 francs per tonne,
and directors Gilson, Dufour and Godwin all profited from helping
the war effort. Business was good even as far away as Caen,
where quarry operators Ambard, Grandory et Grieux 'donated'
stone at seven francs per tonne.

The British soon realized they were paying the French too high
a price for French materials to maintain French roads while helping

to defend France, so granite from Guernsey and the Penlee quarry in Cornwall was shipped to Dunkirk and Boulogne, and quarrying was started by the British at the Lonquety quarry in the Marquise area. This quarry had been operated by German contractors up to the start of the war, but Monsieur Lonquety was delighted to lease it to the British at a royalty of 1.50 francs per tonne.

The need for a geological service for the British Expeditionary Force was apparent early on, and to this end the British Director of Fortifications and Works recruited Lieutenant King of the Royal Welsh Fusiliers. Much advice was given by eminent Belgian and French geologists, and by Major David of the Australian Mining Corps, who had been Professor of Geology at the University of Sydney.

During 1915 and 1916 ten quarry companies were raised in Britain, one in Ireland and two in France, using a workforce

Hasler House was constructed in a house in the village of St Jean for Royal Artillery Battery 93. Care was taken to ensure that the concrete protection for the forward observation officer did not make the structure top-heavy. Despite heavy shelling, Hasler House was still standing at the end of the war.

res-Saint-Jean

Puinen van het oud kasteel van den burgemeester herscha in schuilplaatsen — Ruines de l'ancien château du bourgmestre, transformées en abris

staffed mainly from the quarrying industry in Britain. This workforce was boosted by German prisoners of war, as it was considered that stone-breaking was a useful way for them to pass their time (as well as being a superb source of free labour).

Smaller quantities of materials were obtained by engineering and pioneering companies nearer to the point of use. A Northamptonshire company was shelled whilst working in a small gravel pit behind Ploegsteert Wood in Belgium. Later in the war, a tunnelling company constructing defences around Coigneux in France paid Madame Labis of Orville a royalty of 3.50 francs per cubic metre of sand for the concrete used in her defence and that of the locality in which she lived.

2 *Johnny Get Your Gun* by John F. Tucker (William Kimber Ltd., London 1978).
3 *Permanent Fortifications for the Imperial Military Training Establishments and for the Instruction of Officers of all Arms of the Austro-Hungarian Army* by Major Moritz Ritter von Brunner.
4 Published in June, 1916, in the German official manual *Stellungsbau* (Fieldworks) advising engineers and troops on the advantages and disadvantages of constructing field defences and positions. Later editions updated thinking on shell-proof cover, suggesting reinforced concrete in preference to deep, mined dug-outs.

CHAPTER THREE

British Findings

The geological formation of the Somme, where a major battle was to take place in the summer of 1916, was chalk into which dug-outs and tunnels could be cut without the problems which existed in clay or rock areas, to provide safety and shelter for troops, stores, communications and command. Whilst the Germans took advantage of these conditions, cutting and tunnelling deep into the chalk, the British camped on the surface or took shelter in ruined buildings. The use of solid, reinforced-concrete, shell-proof structures was not considered necessary, and the pill box or concrete machine-gun emplacement as a defensive strategy was yet to be considered, except for a small number of locations where an advantage could be gained by being protected above ground.

Concrete constructions by the British were rare and confined to a small number of observation posts, generally built into existing buildings, to protect artillery observers. Any such structures were the result of local initiatives and consultations between Royal Engineers companies and the divisional artillery, an example being a 30-foot high concrete tower built into the notary's house in Foncquevillers.[5] The construction of permanent protection and

Gibraltar observation post in Pozières village. Looking out to the left of the photograph, it gave good observation over the ridge where the attacking Australians were dug in. (Imperial War Museum E [Aus] 994)

GERMAN SHELL PROOF O.P.

FROM PLAN CAPTURED BY FIFTH ARMY, NOVᴿ 1916.
SCALE 1/25

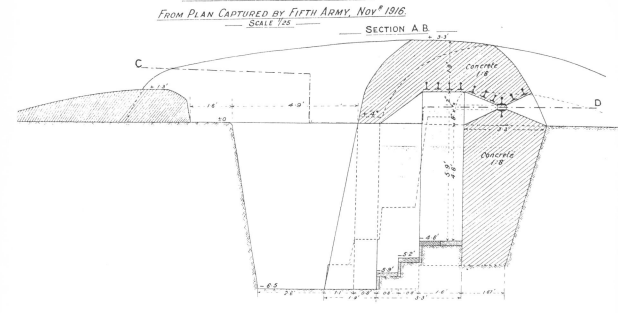

Concrete protection was given to German observers at ground level. This ground-level concrete observation post allowed defenders to see when an attack was starting. This photograph was taken after capture by the British in 1916. Reinforced concrete slabs were used to give strength to weaker and more vulnerable entrances to tunnelled dug-outs.

posts was not considered necessary by higher officials, who expected the front to move forward soon.

In addition to their deep underground shelters, the Germans wanted to provide protection for artillery observation. Observation posts, such as that at Gibraltar on the Pozières ridge, and lower-level posts sited just above parapet level, gave security to the observer. Concrete machine-gun emplacements were not thought necessary, however, as machine-guns were brought out from tunnelled dug-outs when an attack was thought likely and fired over the trench parapet. Such emplacements were few and far between, although historians considered they existed in large numbers:

> ...and one concrete fortlet in the parapet to every fifty yards of front.[6]

Dug-out entrances were weak points in the system and concrete was used to strengthen them. Covered doorways, sometimes incorporated in house foundations, meant that the German soldier was safe during a barrage and could quickly leave his dug-out without facing the problems often posed by collapsed entrances. The construction of concrete doorways and trench entries was complicated, needing excavating and concreting to the required depth before covering over again with earth. Displacing and replacing the chalk also reduced its effective thickness and its ability to withstand shell fire.

A compromise was developed in the laying of a 600mm thick reinforced concrete slab over the dug-out entrance in front of the

To ensure German troops were fed efficiently, field kitchens were constructed to be shell-proof.

trench. The slab was intended to detonate the shell, whilst the chalk below took the force of the explosion. This concept of burster and concussion absorption layers became an integral part of later British thinking in respect of all shell-proof structures.

The Somme battles ground to a halt without the British having considered the use of reinforced concrete on any scale, even though their intelligence service was aware of the large quantities of cement and aggregate being used by the Germans. Pill boxes and bunkers did not play a large part in the battle of the Somme, although the depth and quality of the captured German dug-outs showed the British what that cement and aggregate had been used for, and they were not going to be caught out again. Note was taken of the use of such materials in circumstances where it was advantageous. As further advances towards Berlin were planned, all this information was welcomed by British intelligence. Concrete machine-gun emplacements were known to exist, and the British were familiar with the havoc they could wreak on waves of attacking troops. The breaking-out from Arras, the taking of Vimy Ridge and the subsequent need to smash through the Hindenburg Line helped remind British general staff that concrete was stronger than flesh.

Further north, big events were being planned and yet more information was needed. The concrete bunkers and gun emplacements known to be sited on the Messines Ridge would be undermined by tunnelling companies, but what of those sectors of the German line which could not be mined? British infantry would be attacking German trenches over no-man's-land; British intelligence needed to know what could be expected, and made moves to find out. The 520th (London) Field Company Royal Engineers, attached to the 47th (London) Division which held the line between St Eloi and Hill 60, were given the task and on 20 February, 1917, raided the German trenches accordingly (see map on page 31). The information gained was valuable, indeed so valuable that other engineers of the division were asked to carry out another raid in the same location.

This time the task fell to the 517th (London) Field Company Royal Engineers, accompanied by the 18th Battalion London Regiment. At 7pm on 7 April, 1917, A, B, C and D Companies set off from their trenches, each with a specific objective (see

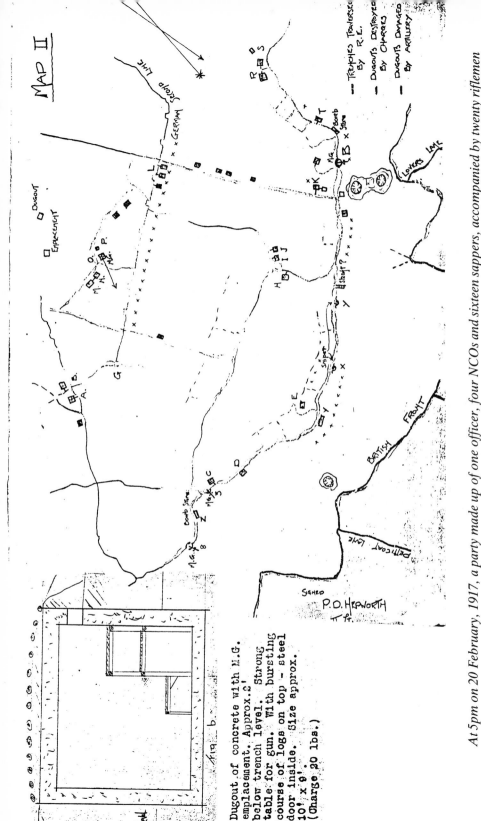

MAP II

— TRENCHES TRAVERSED
BY R.E.

▯ DUGOUTS DESTROYED
BY CHARGES

▮ DUGOUTS DAMAGED
BY ARTILLERY

GERMAN SUPPORT LINE

GERMAN FRONT LINE

LOVERS LANE

Dugout
EMPLACEMENT

BRITISH FRONT

PETTICOAT LANE

M.G. Bomb Store

Sniper

Bomb Store

M.G.

MG Bomb Store

Dugout of concrete with M.G.
emplacement. Approx.2'
below trench level. Strong
table for gun. With bursting
course of logs on top – steel
door inside. Size approx.
10' x 9'.
(Charge 20 lbs.)

Trench level

SIGNED

P.O. HEPWORTH
π Lt.

At 5pm on 20 February, 1917, a party made up of one officer, four NCOs and sixteen sappers, accompanied by twenty riflemen and four companies of infantrymen who were to inflict casualties and take prisoners for intelligence purposes, raided the German trenches opposite Ravine Wood following a heavy artillery barrage. The schedule allowed the raiding party 35 minutes in the German front line, and 15 minutes in their second line. The raid was successful: the enemy's defences were closely examined; and snipers' posts, concrete machine-gun emplacements, bomb stores and dug-outs were mapped and measured, and a number of drawings made. The condition and construction of the trenches was also noted. To let the Germans know of their brief visit, the Royal Engineers detonated ten pounds of guncotton and put paid to a number of bomb stores and other constructions, complete with their contents. The party then retired to the British lines without casualties, despite the attempts of the Germans.

31

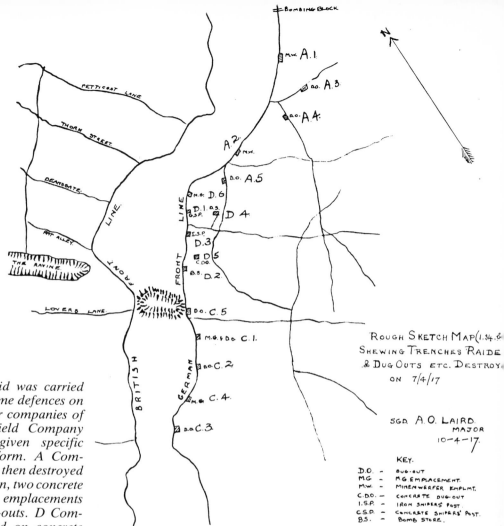

ROUGH SKETCH MAP (1.34.&
SHEWING TRENCHES RAIDE
& DUG OUTS ETC. DESTROY
ON 7/4/17

SGD A. O. LAIRD.
MAJOR
10-4-17.

KEY.

D.O. - DUG-OUT
MG - MG EMPLACEMENT.
M.W. - MINENWERFER EMPLMT.
C.DO. - CONCRETE DUG-OUT
I.S.P. - IRON SNIPERS' POST
C.S.P. - CONCRETE SNIPERS' POST
B.S. - BOMB STORE.

PLANS AND SKETCHES
AS PER REPORTS ATTACHED

A second raid was carried out on the same defences on 7 April. Four companies of the 517th Field Company were each given specific tasks to perform. A Company studied, then destroyed with guncotton, two concrete machine-gun emplacements and two dug-outs. D Company reported on concrete constructions, some made with blocks cemented together and others made with shingle and cement, and all described as 'first class work'. C Company reported that all trenches were badly smashed by artillery, and that dugouts were reinforced with expanded metal or steel bars. In all cases detailed drawings were made of dimensions, locations, depth of cover and door types. B Company Engineers did not report, as they became casualties.

Marked on rough map.

C 1
FIGURE V

map on page 32). On this occasion the Germans were better prepared, however, and the raiders suffered losses.

Raids to gather information on the type and state of the enemy's defences were also carried out by other divisions before the attack on Messines Ridge began. German trenches near Maedelstede Farm, opposite the 16th (Irish) Division, were raided at 8.45pm on 5 April by a party of sixteen Royal Engineers with 270 infantrymen of the 6th Royal Irish Regiment. The raid was succesful, twenty-one prisoners were taken for interrogation and seven dug-outs were inspected and blown up. On the night of 3 June 290 troops of the 6th Connaught Rangers raided Nancy Trench and Nancy Support near Wytschaete; the raid was succesful in that sixty Germans were killed and twenty-four officers and other ranks were taken prisoner. The commanding officer on the raid, Lieutenant Tuite, was awarded the Military Cross for his leadership. The 36th (Ulster) Division carried out a number of raids to gain information, as did the New Zealanders opposite Messines village. On the afternoon of 5 June, less than 48 hours before zero hour, eight sappers of the 1st New Zealand Engineers accompanied an infantry raiding party. On return they recorded:

> heavily concreted dugouts in enemy's front system at La Petite Douve Farm were blown up with gun cotton charges.

The New Zealanders had been watching the progress of the construction of shelters and machine-gun positions throughout May, issuing regular information bulletins and providing information in a daily summary of intelligence. They already had experience of German concrete emplacements, having come up against them in late February whilst in the front line near Fleurbaix: the 2nd Auckland Battalion had raided Fan, Fag, Fly and Fad Trenches on 21 February, 1917, to gain information on the defences and found them to be strong and almost impregnable. Reports were made on the concrete emplacements, some of which were still under construction.

Thus, in the weeks and days before the start of the battle of Messines, the planners received a steady and continuous flow of reports containing detailed information about the nature of German defences and the amount of shell-proof cover provided for troops and machine-gun crews.

Shortly after the reports had been digested, the 19 mines laid under the Messines Ridge exploded, destroying many of the constructions and dug-outs known to exist there. Following the taking of the ridge, and thirsty for more information, intelligence requested further reports. These described monolithic and block constructions and their resistance to shell fire, reporting that some types, mainly solid, unreinforced concrete, shattered fairly easily, while iron joists and rails were found to separate rather than strengthen the concrete. Reinforcement near the surface was noted to be effective both in detonating the shell and helping to prevent splintering inside. The age of different types of constructions was established, identifying the evolution of designs for more efficient protection. Concussion effects were noted and discussed − in a bunker near the Spanbroekmolen crater four German officers were found dead, seated around a table without a wound on any of them.[7]

The success of the battle of Messines, and the wealth of information made available by the preceding trench-raiding activities and subsequent reports, meant up-to-the-minute intelligence was gained on construction methods and the types of deployment of strong defensive positions. British and Australian engineers, field and tunnelling companies and pioneer battalions dissected, analysed, studied and drew the concrete constructions.

The third battle of Ypres opened on 31 July, 1917. The British general staff were convinced that this time its armies could break the stalemate, force the Passchendaele Ridge, and break out to the open country behind it. Imagine the suprise and shock when it was discovered that the enemy had been digging-in for the past two and a half years, constructing:

> a different system of defence... The Germans had built small but very powerful concrete shelters. These were covered with mud and scattered throughout the desert of wet shell holes which stretched in every direction. They were impossible to locate from a distance, and in any case were safe against anything but the very heaviest shells. The farms, most of them surrounded by very broad wet ditches, or moats, had also been heavily concreted within their shattered walls, every one of these was a fort in itself.[8]

HEAVY SHELL PROOF DUGOUT
FOR TWO M.GS. AND CREWS   FROM DOCUMENTS CAPTURED AUGUST 1918.

GERMAN FIELDWORKS

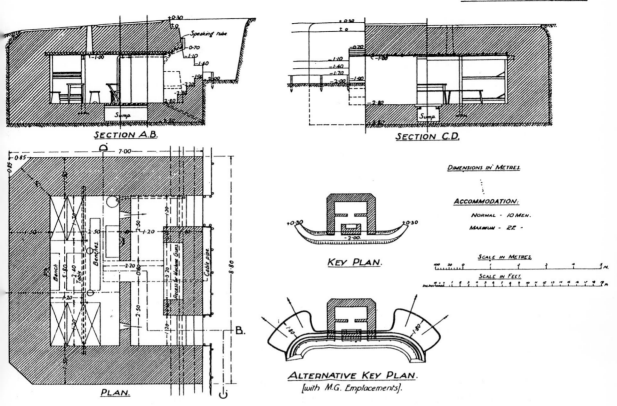

Heavy shell-proof shelters were also constructed to provide protection for troops during a bombardment.

The Germans had indeed been busy. From the front line, right under the noses of the British, to well in the rear, a system of concrete machine-gun emplacements, blockhouses, bunkers, command posts and communications centres had been built. Typical of this new system was Cambrai Trench, located in front of Wieltje, with pill boxes and bunkers standing almost shoulder-to-shoulder, all built to a similar design and all developed to protect infantry from pre-attack bombardment.

Behind the front line almost every farmhouse and outbuilding was concreted, many sited in strategic positions and generally in clusters, giving each other covering fire. Only a minority of emplacements had loop-holes for machine-guns, most being

35

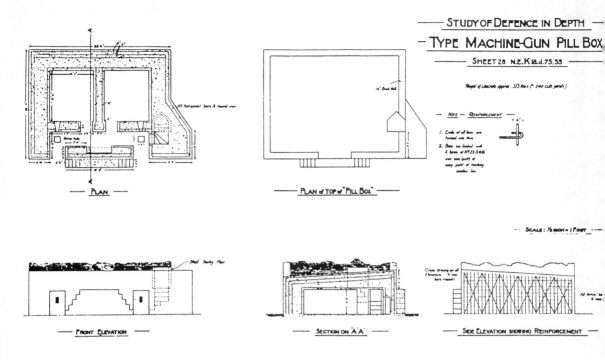

PLAN

PLAN of TOP of "PILL BOX"

FRONT ELEVATION

SECTION ON "A A"

SIDE ELEVATION SHOWING REINFORCEMENT

To ease construction difficulties, and following earlier findings on design faults, the Germans produced a number of standard designs of pill boxes. Most were shell-proof bunkers, with machine-guns being fired over the roof. A design used for many constructions in the forward and rear areas in front of Ypres had shell-proof chambers for the machine-gun operators (above), several of which still exist in the Menin-Moorslede area (below). Due to the rapidity of the Allied advance in September 1918, many were captured with relative ease. The Menin-Moorslede area was at the junction of the Belgian and British Armies (opposite above) with both the Belgian and the British (9th Scottish, 29th and 34th Divisions) capturing examples. The bunker in the Dadizeele Military Cemetery (opposite bottom), built to this design, is used as a storage hut by the cemetery gardeners.

'blind': shelters for machine-gun crews who would mount their guns and fire over the top.

The use of pre-cast blocks was common, including both holed and grooved patterns produced at a factory in Wervik, plus plain blocks used as burster courses over plain concrete. A block arch construction on Sterling Castle ridge was typical of the diversity of styles, the blocks also being used as walls to support reinforced concrete roofs.[9]

All were solid, without a separating air layer. Most could withstand all but a direct hit from a heavy shell, and even then the quality of concrete and the reinforcement — small, closely-centred rods rather than rails — meant that many suffered only minor exterior damage. The occupants could safely sit out a bombardment, although the danger of concrete flaking off inside on impact and the effects of concussion led to many casualties.

The pill boxes and bunkers proved difficult to capture, as heavy bombardment often made the ground around difficult to cross. Nevertheless, successful tactical methods were devised to overcome the problem and, yet again, the Royal Engineers followed the attackers to provide even more reports for intelligence. As with the previous reports, styles, materials, strengths and weaknesses were noted and discussed.

General Headquarters considered the bunkers to be rather too popular with the British troops, and not as effective as reported. The summary of information dated 6 August, 1917, stated that concrete dug-outs were not popular with the Germans, were dangerous and to be avoided, and many were reserved for officers. The summary of information of 7 August reported from a captured German order that the concrete dug-outs between Pilkem and St Julien had all been 'destroyed or rendered unserviceable'. This was news to the British Tommies sheltering 200 yards away, who would no doubt have been willing to offer their contribution to such 'informative' reports.

Protection for German soldiers and their command services had been provided from the front line to reserve lines eight miles to the rear. The shelters ranged in size from small machine-gun emplacements holding three or four men, up to quarters holding several hundred, including the all-important headquarters, hospitals and kitchens.

In the Ypres Salient, from the Pilkem Ridge down to Hill 60, the number of concrete constructions totalled over 2,000. Many were in groups, and were used either to provide supporting fire for each other or as administrative centres. A great number were destroyed in the 1917 fighting, but when the Germans swept back to their old positions in April and May, 1918, over 1,200 were still habitable and usable.

Having seen the effectiveness of these concrete emplacements on the attacker, the British decided, at last, to investigate them officially. In the critical periods of late 1917 and early 1918 intelligence discovered that, whilst the infantry were demanding protection from high explosive, they and the Royal Engineers companies actually had the knowledge and ability to provide it. Much had been gained by studying captured German constructions and plans, in some cases blowing them up deliberately to investigate the effects. Moreover, some Royal Engineers companies had already built bunkers and machine-gun emplacements. General Headquarters decided to pool this

Some existing pill boxes − both British and German − were deliberately damaged to assess and measure the effects.

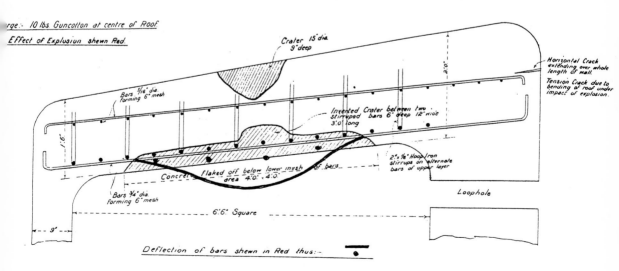

REPORT OF TEST ON REINFORCED CONCRETE M.G. EMPLACEMENT
KEMMEL, DEC.R 7th 1917.

The size and amount of reinforcing steel was very important; concrete that shattered was very dangerous for the troops inside.

knowledge to see how designs and methods of construction could be improved upon.

From earlier studies the thickness of cover needed for protection from shell fire was known, as was the preference for small rods as opposed to railway girders for reinforcement. What was not fully understood was the manner in which an explosive shell could penetrate concrete and disrupt steel reinforcement, nor how the steel performed under such impact.

It was decided that shell hits upon British and captured German constructions should be studied, and the resulting information used to improve designs. The effects of placing steel reinforcing rods on the outer and inner face and midway between were compared, as was the thickness of the steel. Large numbers of small diameter rods, rather than a smaller number of thicker ones, proved more protective. Steel on the outer face helped limit the depth of penetration; as the effects of a shell splintering the

CONCRETE MACHINE-GUN EMPLACEMENT.

Scale $\frac{3}{16}'' = 1'$.

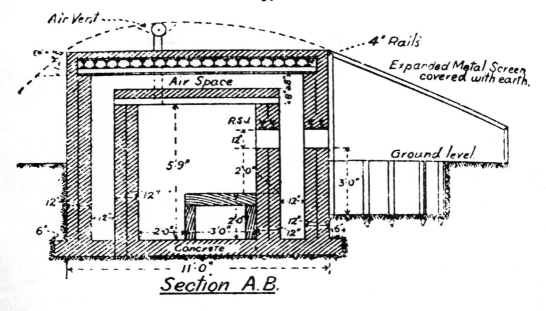

Designs for shell-proof pill boxes with air pockets to absorb concussion were produced, but were impractical to construct in the field.

inner face was extremely dangerous to the inhabitants, closely spaced, small diameter steel rods, known to be successful in holding together concrete, were used for this purpose. Wire mesh (chicken wire) and expanded metal worked even better. Concussion effects had proved fatal and it was considered that an air gap within the concrete thickness would help to minimize it. The 'perfect' design was determined as a well-reinforced concrete outer skin to set the fuse and cause the shell to explode, with an inner reinforced concrete skin to protect the inhabitants, the two layers being separated by an air space of about six inches to absorb the explosion.

A number of designs were produced, but the problems of building a two-layer construction while keeping the two skins apart were not fully considered or appreciated. Supports to the outer skin during construction were found to transmit forces to the inner skin, thus negating the advantage of air space. In some

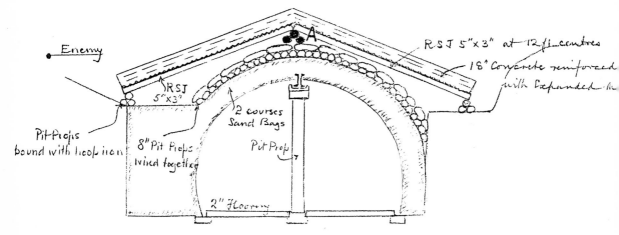

Labels in the drawing:
Enemy
RSJ 5"x3" at 12 ft. centres
18" Concrete reinforced with Expanded M...
RSJ 5"x3"
2 courses Sand Bags
Pit Props bound with hoop iron
8" Pit Props wired together
Pit Prop
2" Flooring
A

Practicalities of construction and values of the air space were considered by field engineers. It was found difficult to support the outer layer during construction, as any supports transmitted the shock of the explosion to the inner skin, thus negating the value of the air pocket. In this example drawn by a Royal Engineer constructing a company headquarters in Oxford Terrace near Givenchy, he considered 'that the value of the air space is largely wasted, because all the shock taken by the superior roof is transmitted to the inferior roof by the central support of the former' (the three pit props at A). A later development was to use a layer of soft earth in place of the air space, thus supporting the outer skin whilst absorbing the concussion.

circumstances a thick layer of soft earth was found to be effective in absorbing the concussion. Much of the work on perfecting the design and studying the practicalities of incorporating the air space was carried out in field conditions by the Royal Engineers.

5 Described in *My Sapper Venture* by Lieutenant-Colonel V. F. Eberle, a Royal Engineers officer with the 48th South Midland Division (Pitman, 1973).
6 *The Battle of the Somme* by John Masefield (Heinemann, 1919). The author was more than a little enthusiastic about the strength of German defences.
7 *German Concrete Structures on Messines Ridge and the Effect of Shell Fire on them.* See Appendix 1.
8 *The Fifth Army* by General Sir Hubert Gough (Chivers, London, reprinted 1968).
9 *German Concrete Structures in the Area North of Ypres, Captured in August 1917, and the Effect of Shell Fire on them.* See Appendix 2.

Chapter Four

Difficult Conditions

The logistical problems of producing large monolithic structures in or near the front line were readily apparent. Sand and ballast was much in demand for filling sandbags, providing dry material for trench bottoms and filling shell-holes in the pavé roads, but it was in constant competition for transport with other supplies such as food, general stores and ammunition. Added to this was the constant problem of keeping cement dry. However, one of the major problems was in mixing and placing the concrete without noise or, in the case of night work, without light.

In mid-1916 German maps were captured, with the word Mischplätze (mixing places) marked alongside trench tramways. These Mischplätze were presumed to be the nightly destinations of large carrying and working parties. The Second Army daily intelligence summary[10] dated 2 November, 1916, stated that, apart from bringing up cement and aggregate to the front line, concrete blocks were being made at pioneer parks behind the front and used for the construction of rear lines and gun emplacements.[11] This was felt to be a fairly new development, as the German official manual Stellungsbau, in the secret *Cover from Shell Fire* document dated June, 1916, mentioned only monolithic concrete, although it was known that blocks had been in use since March, 1916.[12]

The German army area with the greatest need was in Flanders. A concrete block factory was established at Wervik in Belgium, which had the advantage of being located on the River Lys and linked to the trench tramway system serving the front around the Ypres Salient. It was discovered that the use of plain, brick-shaped blocks limited the advantages of the system: they were ideal for forming inner and outer walls to receive a reinforced concrete core, but the absence of reinforcement between the blocks severely reduced the resistance to shell damage.

The Wervik factory produced blocks of a design which allowed

German military and Belgian civilian workers produced concrete blocks to be connected with steel rods for strength. (Imperial War Museum Q 45472)

Blocks, with sand and cement for jointing mortar, were taken on trench railways through Zandvoorde to front line positions. (Imperial War Museum Q 45545)

A block-built bunker after being taken near Polygon Wood on 21 September, 1917. The solidity of the system is illustrated by the way the blocks have held together when hit by a shell. (Imperial War Museum E [Aus] 775)

A similar bunker today, again showing relatively little damage to the corner.

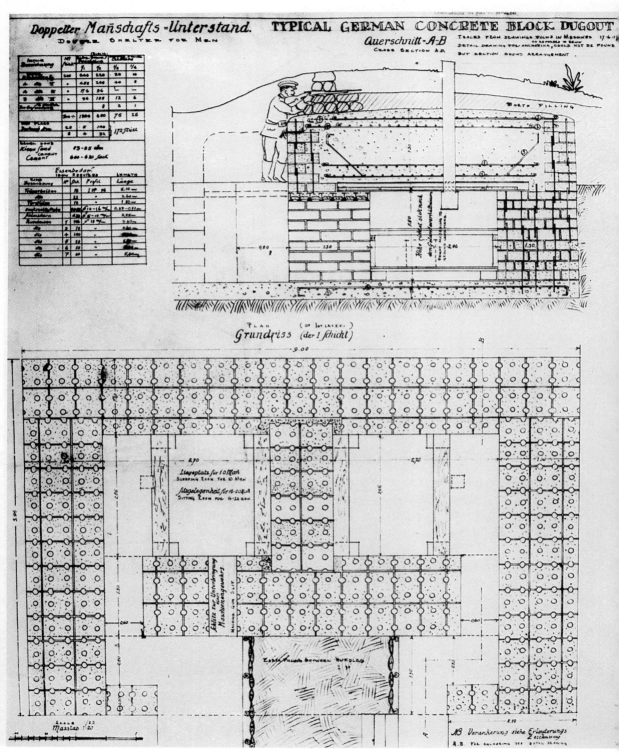

A captured plan shows how the blocks were used to construct the walls. A solid, reinforced-concrete roof was then cast.

reinforcement bars to pass between and through the blocks. This enabled a wide range of structural designs to be built which, when threaded with steel and cemented with a cement and sand mortar, were almost as strong as solid reinforced concrete. Similar designs were adopted by other factories in the occupied territories.

After the taking of the Messines Ridge various British field companies were given the opportunity to study a number of these concrete structures at leisure.[13] It was found that the earlier ones were made of plain blocks, with steel joists and rails in the roof. Later versions were made of blocks with one-inch diameter holes, two through the centre line of the block and four semicircular holes in the longer sides. Reports on their resistance to shell fire were contradictory. The 250th Tunnelling Company reported that:

> this form of shelter is practically immune from shell fire, 80 per cent of these shelters examined were undamaged, although the entrances were blocked up in all cases.

A report from another company stated:

> It was seen that in some instances structures of solid concrete had resisted our shell fire, but, where concrete blocks were used, in many instances the structure was knocked over in such a way as to render it useless and a trap for the occupants.

After the third Ypres battles the engineer-in-chief summarized reports from the field companies, stating that monolithic concrete had stood up well to bombardment. The block system of construction was condemned, however, as 'All dug-outs built of concrete blocks that were hit were done in'. It was not surprising that, coupled with its 'offensive' policy and, given that concrete shelters were not considered a good idea, the British were not quick in following the German example of using pre-cast blocks.

With the expected change of position before the Americans arrived in force, and the Germans taking the offensive, British thinking was beginning to change. Consideration was given in late 1917 to the construction of block structures, leaning on what little experience had been gained from using small blocks for dug-outs built in Sanctuary Wood.

In late 1917 the British First Army developed a concrete pill box system for easy erection in the battle zone. A factory was built in Aire-sur-la-Lys to produce the blocks and beams for these pill boxes, several of which can still be found in France. The

The First Army, covering the northern edge of the Forest of Nieppe down to Arras, were the first off the mark when the British started constructing concrete pill boxes. In September, 1917, the 230th Field Company Royal Engineers started working on plans for a large pre-cast pill box factory, with a school of instruction attached. Aire-sur-la-Lys, a busy Royal Engineers locality with excellent water and rail links, was chosen as the factory site. Limestone from the Marquise quarries and sand and cement in wooden barrels were shipped in by barge and off-loaded into storage hoppers. After processing, the blocks and beams were loaded on to railway trucks for transporting to field engineer companies. The blocks were strengthened with expanded metal, and had holes for threading reinforcing bars. Roof beams had reinforcing bars and stirrups, and were designed to be bonded and tied in with the blocks. The construction method was quick and simple: walls were built dry with the steel rods threaded; the joints were then pointed on the inside and outside faces, and a wet cement grout poured down special vertical holes to grout in the steel bars. The early ones had a major design fault, in that the wet cement grout penetrated only to the top few courses of blocks, leaving the rest loose-laid. To overcome this problem later ones were grouted as the walls went up. The School of Concrete began its first course for the Royal Artillery on 23 January, 1918, concluding it on 12 February. The following day the next course started, lasting only fourteen days (which became the standard length for instruction courses). Production and instruction continued until 11 April, 1918, when all available hands had to be despatched to help stem the German breakthrough. Production restarted on 30 April, continuing until 7 November. When at its peak in June and July, 1918, the Aire-sur-la-Lys factory production was over 7,000 wall blocks and up to 700 roof beams a day.

CONCRETE BLOCK "PILL BOX".

STANDARD DESIGN.

Walls and roof 3'9" thick.
Weight of block 52 lbs.
Weight of beam 300 lbs.

NOTE—Size of Pill Box 6'0" wide. Length to be in
multiples of 1'6" to retain same bonding
Drawing shows Pill Box 13'6" long.

Outside face of block

Detail of Wall block

Spiral stirruping fastened to
horizontal bars with malleable
wire as shown.

Detail of Beam
Showing reinforcement.

Nº	TOTAL NET QUANTITIES	WEIGHT	
		TONS	CWT
3902	Wall Blocks	90	11
68	Half Blocks		16
392	Beams	52	10
336	Rods (4' long, hooked over beams)		8
990	Rods (4' 6" long		6
12	Cubic Yds. Sand for grouting	1	9
40	Barrels of Cement for "	4	3
	Total weight	767	3

Wall blocks on edge

Spaces between beams
top course to be filled
with wall blocks on...

Isometric view.

Spaces between beams in bottom course
to be filled in with wall blocks on edge.

Second Army, to the north of the First, studied the Aire-sur-la-Lys factory block system, made improvements, and started producing blocks at Arques, south of St Omer in France, in a factory already producing concrete floor slabs, drainpipes and so on. The Arques block was not reinforced but had cast-in channels to facilitate the introduction of steel rods placed horizontally and vertically. A reinforced roof-beam was also produced (see below).

As both designs were promoted as being superior to the other, a complete set of each was shipped across the English Channel to the artillery grounds at Shoeburyness in Essex. Comparative trials were carried out on 21 August, 1918. It was found that both structures were resistant to a 5.9″ shell at low range. The Aire-sur-la-Lys pattern suffered more damage due to its lack of lateral reinforcement, but the expanded metal in the blocks minimized the concussion and concrete flaking inside. Although the Arques pattern was stronger, its concrete flaked off inside

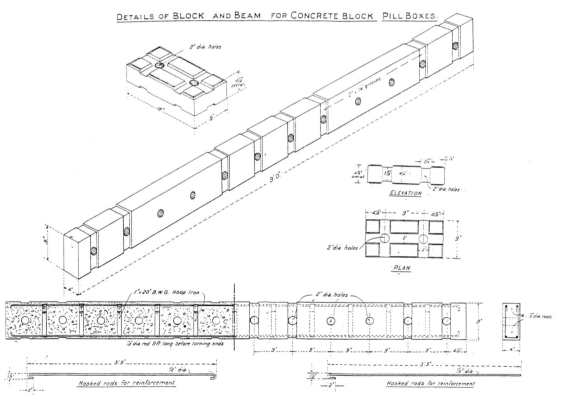

Second Army beams and blocks were of a different pattern, but still allowed interlocking for strength.

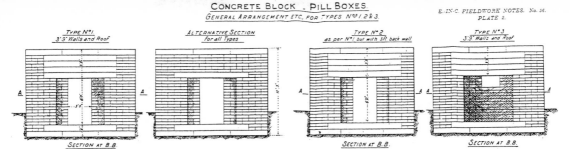

CONCRETE BLOCK . PILL BOXES.
GENERAL ARRANGEMENT ETC, FOR TYPES Nos 1 2 & 3.

E.-IN-C. FIELDWORK NOTES. No. 56.
PLATE 2.

TYPE Nº 1.
3'9" Walls and Roof

ALTERNATIVE SECTION
For all Types

TYPE Nº 2.
as per Nº 1 but with 3ft. back wall

TYPE Nº 3.
3'9" Walls and Roof

SECTION AT B.B.   SECTION AT B.B.   SECTION AT B.B.

The Second Army also produced standard designs for concrete block pill boxes.

A Second Army pattern pill box nearing completion of its camouflage.

An example of a Second Army style pill box constructed near Hazebrouck.

51

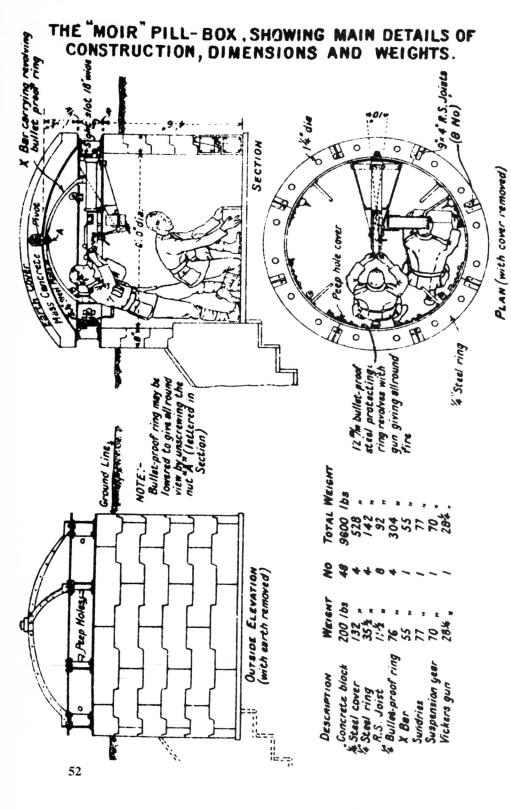

The Moir pill box as conceived by Sir Ernest Moir, with concrete blocks cast by the Royal Engineers in Richborough, Kent, and metal works supplied by civilian manufacturers. The kit was sent to France or any other destination ready for assembly. Winston Churchill liked the idea, was persuaded by his advisers that it would be worthwhile, and gave approval for production to proceed.

and its lack of internal reinforcement caused much wastage. The trials suggested the ideal combination: the shape of the Arques type with the internal reinforcement of the Aire-sur-la-Lys model.

Whilst these pre-cast ideas were being formulated, the boffins in Whitehall were also busy. Sir Ernest Moir of the Ministry of Munitions was granted an indenture for Secret Patent No. 88 for the Moir pill box, a six-feet interior diameter circular concrete block wall supporting a steel dome from which was suspended a revolving steel bullet-proof ring and a machine-gun. It was intended to be proof against field-gun fire, or a 5.9″ shell exploding not less than three feet away. A prototype was demonstrated in the safety of Kensington Gardens, London. Winston Churchill, then Minister of Munitions, inspected it, was duly impressed, ordered 500, and went to lunch.

A total of about 1,500 Moir pill boxes were eventually produced. The system of concrete blocks in a curved shape with interlocking sections for rigidity when fixed was quite advanced for the time; earlier systems using Winget concrete block machinery had produced only rectangular blocks with central holes. Casting was carried out at Richborough on the Kent coast, the Royal Engineers' main base and port. Large sand and gravel deposits gave easy supplies of aggregate, and a large concrete block casting

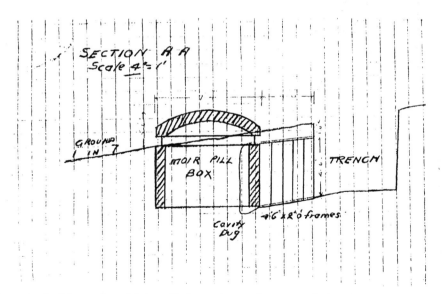

A typical siting of a Moir pill box, located at trench level giving a protected emplacement with good observation and field of fire. The sketch was drawn in a pocket book by a Royal Engineer siting it near Ypres.

works was already operated there by the Royal Engineers for accommodation buildings.

Contracts were placed with Messrs Braithwaite of West Bromwich for the steel girders and cupolas, and with Vickers for the machine-gun mountings. Each pill box kit comprised 48 concrete blocks, metal girders, four domed roof sections, a bullet-proof ring, bolts and fixings, a gun mounting and an ammunition-box carrier. It also included the necessary sand and cement, five-eighths of an inch reinforcing rods for the roof, camouflage stores and a set of the correct tools: masons' hammers and trowels, 'level, field, R.E.', 'frames, carrying, for blocks (four men)', as well as sundry items like spanners, picks and 'grease, tins of − 1'.

It was calculated that each pill box required four lorries for transportation. Once a Royal Engineers or other officer had selected the site the labour requirement was:

NCOs   One Corporal knowledgeable of setting-out, levelling, etc
       One Lance Corporal, a fitter

Men   One Mason
      One Fitter's mate
      Eight Labourers (all must be strong men).

Erection instructions were detailed and precise, describing excavation, foundation work, levelling, the use of templet, building up of blocks, the fitting and correcting of the domed roof, and camouflage including the obliteration of footmarks and paths round about.

The majority of the Moir pill box sets were sent from Richborough to various sectors of the Western Front, with locations from Amiens in the south to Ypres in the north. A further 379 were ordered for British coastal defences, and twenty-five were sent to Salonica. Royal Engineers companies in the field were given practical instructions in the erection of the Moir pill box. Companies such as the 237 Field Company, while improving defences in front of Scherpenberg, were able to fit up trial sections at Royal Engineers dumps before erection in the lines.

The Moir pill box itself was designed to be positioned below ground level, with the observation/machine-gun steel shield rising about nine inches above ground level. The total height of the structure was about two feet, with the entrance and occupants at trench level. Where conditions dictated, the pill box was constructed at ground level and stood about seven feet high. In these circumstances an extra layer of concrete, twelve inches thick with light mesh reinforcement, was advised. Later specifications for siting gave the height of the loop-hole 'to be not less than eighteen inches above the ground'. In addition, four-inch-diameter holes were ordered to be cut into the steel cupola roof 'until the parabolic cups (for gas emission from the machine gun) have been issued and found to be satisfactory'. Following initial problems with water, instructions were given to provide satisfactory drainage, usually into the adjoining trench.

The summer of 1918 saw large numbers of Moir pill boxes erected in the defence lines in France and Flanders, mainly in the northern sector where Royal Engineers companies were receiving and erecting them up to the start of October. On 23 October, when the Allied advance in the north was progressing and it

The original design of the Moir Pill Box was for the machine gun embrasure to be at ground level. In some case where trenches were built up with sand bags rather than dug, extra strength could be given by casting a layer of concrete around the outside. This example, constructed as part of the West Hazebrouck Line in the summer of 1918, shows the rear doorway; the revolving visor has been removed. It can be found close to Cinq Rues cemetery, on the N42.

A Moir pill box, constructed as part of the West Hazebrouck Line, showing the revolving steel bullet-proof plate and machine-gun embrasure.

seemed likely that the end of the war was imminent, all orders for Moir pill boxes were cancelled.

In January, 1919, 730 complete sets were still sitting in the Richborough Royal Engineers port area. Some Moir pill boxes are still in evidence today. Two very good examples, erected by the 208th Field Company Royal Engineers for the 34th Division, can be seen on the ramparts at Ypres. Others, forming part of the old West Hazebrouck Line, can be seen between Hazebrouck and Wallon Cappel.

A design favoured by the Australians, probably because it was designed by the Australians, was the Hobbs pill box. The idea was conceived by Major-General J. Talbot Hobbs, commander of the 5th Australian Division, who had noted the benefits of protected machine-gun emplacements at Bullecourt in May, 1917, and Polygon Wood, Ypres in September, 1917. The Hobbs pill box consisted of an armour-plated cupola which revolved on six rollers with an attached machine gun, all supported by armour steel sheeting. Designed to be buried in the earth with just the cupola and firing slits above ground level, it offered space only for a machine-gun operator and loader. Its total weight was 17cwt, two quarters and 26 pounds. Extra protection against near misses

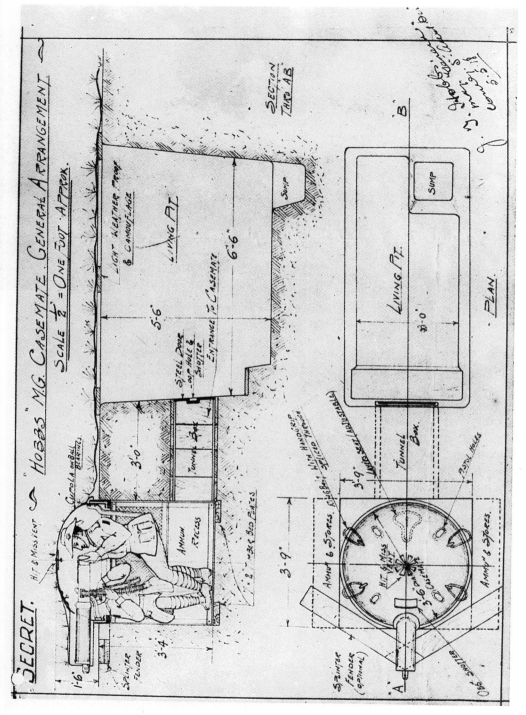

The Australian designed Hobbs Machine Gun Casement could be used in earth or concrete.

was provided by a concrete floor and the encasement of the walls in concrete.

A total of 257 Hobbs pill boxes were produced by the North British Locomotive Company and Messrs Beardmore in Glasgow. Of these, 210 were sent to France and Belgium, sited mainly in Australian sectors. The remaining forty-seven were still in Glasgow on 8 November, 1918, and were then classed as 'of no military value' and were considered for re-smelting. Of those used in France and Belgium, none have survived, probably because of the scrap value of the metal.

Another Australian design showing a deal of imagination and inventive on-the-spot thinking was developed by Captain Webb of the 7th Field Company, Australian Engineers. While constructing observation posts in the Ploegsteert area in January, 1918, he started to use standard-issue 'elephant' steel shelters as a means of producing circular posts. By laying these shelters on their sides and infilling with concrete he constructed what was to become the standard design Webb observation post.

After the successful use of concrete in fortifying observation posts in the Ypres Salient during 1915 and 1916, the British decided to expand this practice to monitoring troop movements, battery plotting, general observation and artillery spotting.

Many structures were adapted to suit. The brickworks at Wulpen, headquarters of the 126th (East Lancashire) Brigade and the Royal Engineers 428 Field Company during October, 1917, had a high chimney which provided an excellent vantage point. It was concreted in such a way that it could be scaled from inside or out, and was sufficiently strong to withstand a direct hit on its top edge. Other engineer companies in the area were also active, with the 148 Army Troops Company constructing observation posts in buildings at Ramskapelle and Pervyse. (This company enjoyed the rare distinction of being one of the very few to be supplied with a petrol-driven concrete mixer. It was delivered on 29 October, 1917, a date which the troops mixing concrete by hand remembered with gratitude.)

The Germans in the area were also building similar high viewpoint structures. The village of Klerken was sited on a slight rise and the roof of a house in the village square gave a perfect view of several miles over and beyond Belgian and British lines.

The brickworks (stonebakkery) chimney at Wulpen gave excellent views over the flat Flanders plain.

The German observation tower at Klerken gave observation behind the Allied lines almost to the coast, allowing full information about movements to be gained. Well camouflaged inside a building, it was hidden from view until shell fire removed the external brick cladding. Although withstanding direct hits from Allied shells, it could not withstand progress and unfortunately was demolished in 1990.

A good example of a concrete structure cast within an existing house, on top of Aubers Ridge overlooking the British lines and connected to the artillery command centre.

It was three stories high, well camouflaged, and sufficiently well constructed to take a large shell just below observer-slit level without major damage.

Other buildings were concreted and strengthened at various positions on the Western Front; whilst the height of two- and three-storey buildings was an obvious advantage, single-storey buildings were an asset in the right location. A house on top of Aubers Ridge gave excellent views over the British lines between Neuve Chapelle and Laventie. Still there today, its design incorporates a telephone room, excellent camouflage and inventive use of mesh reinforcement.

Where height could not be utilized, and where forward positions did not permit the mixing of large amounts of concrete, the Germans developed a number of factory-made, almost ready-for-use, low-level observation posts. These circular steel structures, snail shells, could be rolled into position, then covered

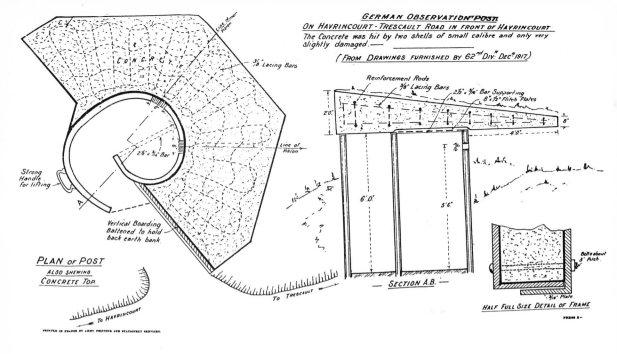

The German 'snail shell' steel observation post was designed to be rolled into position and then given a strengthening covering of concrete. Found in Havrincourt Wood, this one was reported on by the 62nd Division.

This observation post still exists in Havrincourt Wood.

with a thin layer of concrete for strengthening. A similar easy-to-erect design incorporated steel plates bolted together, with a bull-nose steel bullet-proof front giving good cover to a front-line observer.

Protection from shell fire was equally as important well behind the front line. Command and communications centres were liable to severe disruption unless assured of strong protection from bombardment, and, for both the British and the Germans, reinforced concrete played an ever more important role. The Germans constructed strong, solid bunkers resistant to heavy shells for many battalion and division headquarters, in addition to infantry bunkers in the front line area and just to the rear. Because of the organizational effects of a direct hit on a command bunker (and because officers were deemed to need more protection than soldiers), the minimum of one metre thickness of reinforced concrete for these shelters was often doubled, as was the thickness of the walls, and the quality of construction was improved. More attention was given to their appearance, particularly to the entrances, which often had the constructors' personalized name-plate cast into the wall. Details such as wall copings and renderings were added by pioneer companies wishing to show pride in their handiwork.

Dressing stations and field hospitals were built to be shell-proof, ranging from 'only-just-shell-proof' first aid posts, to the 'heaviest-of-shell-proof' dressing stations where medical officers were able to work in a well-lit and ventilated environment.

Equally as important, and certainly more popular, was the field kitchen. Whereas cooking was generally an open-air activity, during periods of bombardment the only way to ensure that the troops were fed was by protecting the kitchen staff. Standard designs did not apply to field kitchens, as any bunker with a store and chimney could be adapted for cooking purposes – bunkers, shelters, and so on were frequently adapted during their construction to incorporate cooking facilities.

The British made less use of large concrete constructions for unit headquarters (being, of course, always ready to move closer to Berlin at the drop of a hat). However, it was accepted that medical requirements for the wounded could not wait that long, and in some sectors concrete dressing stations were constructed.

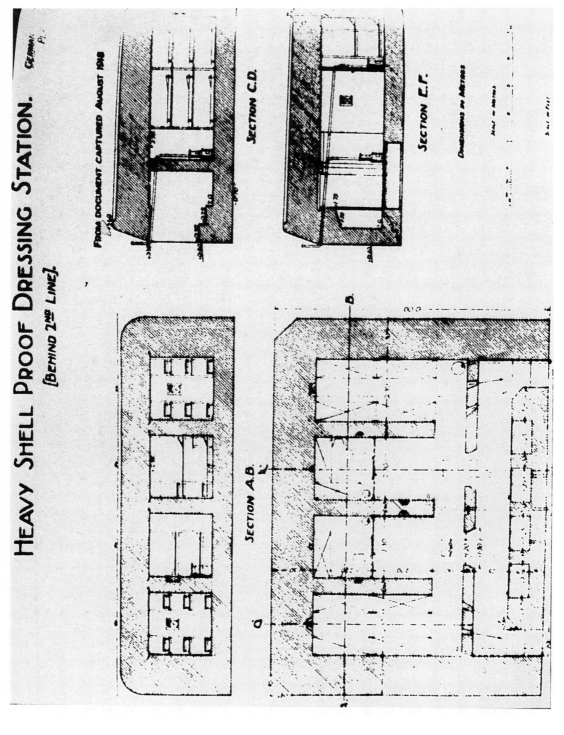

Heavy shell-proof dressing stations were constructed to protect German medical officers and their patients. The labour and materials required by such dressing stations were substantial.

Concrete field kitchens were constructed to ensure that food supplies would always be available for the troops.

First aid stations, such as Blighty Hall in Ploegsteert Wood, were shrapnel- and splinter-proof, although not protected against a direct hit from a field gun.

Stronger and safer field hospitals were built at selected locations for the care of the wounded. Essex Farm in the Yser Canal embankment between Ypres and Boesinghe is a good example of a small concrete hospital design – though it has been used as a cow-byre and tool shed in recent years. Whilst its structure, and therefore its capacity to withstand a direct hit, is weakened by the lack of reinforcing steel, allowing natural stresses from the surrounding earth to snap the framework, walls and floor slabs, the apparent quality of workmanship is high. The quality of concrete, reflected by lack of deterioration, clean arrises and details, is rather higher than the structural condition would suggest; the interior, with blue fleurs-de-lis stencilled on the white walls, shows the efforts sometimes made to create a civilized environment.

Essex Farm was part of a continuous line of dug-outs tunnelled into the whole length of the embankment stretching from Ypres to beyond Boesinghe. The advanced dressing station there was developed over 1915 and 1916 into a large centre for the accommodation of patients and stores. Smaller bunkers 250 yards further up the embankment were manned by the 129 Field Ambulance of the 38th (Welsh) Division.

In late June, 1917, immediately before the start of the third Ypres battle, the bunkers at Essex Farm included the provision of shell-proof buildings for two motor ambulances used by the 133 Field Ambulance. On 22 June it was taken over by detachments of the 1/3 Highland Field Ambulance attached to the 51st (Highland) Division, who were due to attack over the Pilkem Ridge towards St Julien. It was heavily shelled on 10 July, causing much damage — eight stretcher-bearers were buried in one dug-out, and the motor ambulance was damaged.

Other field hospitals were constructed to be shell-proof prior to the expected battles. On 24 February, 1917, in preparation for the Messines offensive, 520th (Field) Company, together with a working party from the 6th London Field Ambulance, Royal Army Medical Corps, started work on Woodcote House, between Bedford House and Shrapnel Corner. The 520th's history gives an interesting account of work:

The farm consisted of four long buildings, surrounding a particularly unsavoury midden, so that, although under observation by the enemy, work could be carried on by day within the farm without its being noticed. The work itself was the construction of shell-proof accommodation in the farm buildings for a dressing station, consisting of a reception room, operating room, and stretcher space for forty-eight stretchers; also an officers' ward, stores, and billets for the RAMC personnel employed. The rooms when completed consisted almost entirely of cupola shelters (both elephant and large British) standing longitudinally within the buildings on low brick walls, and covered with 18 inches of concrete. Above this came an air space, and then two feet of concrete, carried by girders let into the side walls of the buildings; over this again was nine inches of earth, and finally a bursting course of concrete blocks. Work was carried out at Woodcote Farm for three months, the accommodation for personnel being made by the 4th RWF (Pioneers)   [1/4th Battalion,

Royal Welsh Fusiliers], whilst the remainder of this work was done by this Company. Owing to a disappointing falling off in the cement supply towards the end, the job was not quite finished, though very nearly so. The billets in the farm were at first poor, but we gradually moved into the concreted cupolas as they were completed, and by the time the attentions of the enemy got really unpleasant all men were able to find shell-proof cover in case of emergency.

As the battles of Messines and third Ypres pushed the British front line further eastwards, advanced dressing stations and regimental aid posts also moved forwards. Although still liable to receive attention from the enemy, the pill boxes, bunkers and dug-outs taken from them were used extensively by medical teams. Other units also had need of what were the only solid structures in a shell-formed landscape. Battalion and company headquarters and signals and field artillery crews all wanted them. They were generally surrounded by mud, flooded, or damaged by shell fire and, if occupied by medical teams as was usually the case, overflowing with wounded. Other aid posts were constructed up and down the front, mainly one- or two-cupola centres for first aid use only. As with infantry bunkers, the general staff did not want troops to get too settled or dug in, as it was always hoped that the line would shortly be moving eastwards.

10 Produced for dissemination of intelligence to corps, divisions, and so on.
11 Engineer-in-chief *Field Work* Notes No. 7.
12 It was known that both military and civilian labour was used.
13 *German Concrete Structures on Messines Ridge and the Effect of Shell Fire on Them.* See Appendix 1.

CHAPTER FIVE

External and Internal

With the intelligence reports received by British planners in early 1917, information from defences captured in earlier battles — the Somme, Arras, Bullecourt — and information gleaned from German prisoners, it was known that the forthcoming campaigns to capture Messines Ridge and the land beyond the Ypres Salient would encounter many positions which would be likely to hold up an infantry attack. A constant stream of information from diverse sources — trench raids, captured documents, engineers' reports, the known importation of huge amounts of concrete materials into Flanders — confirmed that defences were both strong and in depth, going back for many kilometres behind the front line.

The French, who had already conducted major investigations of German constructions, provided yet more detailed information to the British. Much of this was public knowledge: the French magazine *L'Illustration* in January, 1917, contained detailed reports on concrete dug-outs captured in 1916. On 14 April the same magazine carried details and photographs of *in situ* and pre-cast bunkers under construction. The photographs had been taken from a captured German officer.

The effectiveness of shell-proof concrete shelters in stopping or slowing an attack was increasingly found to be a problem. Some British commanders acknowledged this, and trained troops in methods of attacking these posts, although objective lines were often drawn up with the presumption that little delay and few casualties would be caused. Pill boxes were captured during the first days of the 1917 Messines and Ypres battles by troops using hurriedly devised tactics. The Australians on Messines Rige found that ths 'blockhoue fighting' was especially ferocious. Their official history, describing the first instances of pill-box fighting, records:

> They will kill until they grow tired of killing. When
> they have been racked with machine-gun fire, the

routing out of enemy groups from behind several feet of concrete is almost invariably the signal for butchery at least of the first few who emerge, and sometimes even the helplessly wounded may not be spared.[14]

Tactics were refined during the later stages of the fighting. Artillery was often used to provide a barrage, sometimes including smoke shells, behind which troops could proceed, aiming to arrive before the Germans inside the shelters had time to emerge. On occasions, in wet conditions, these barrages aided the defenders by making the surrounding ground impassable.

Troops practised and rehearsed procedures to tackle pill boxes and blockhouses, sometimes with good success. But the effectiveness of camouflage, the resistance of the structures to shell fire, the tenacity of the defenders and the planners' insistence on keeping to rigid timetables still caused many casualties. Repeated attempts, often ending in failure and the deaths of the attackers, were ordered to tackle strongpoints which held up the infantry.

Concrete machine-gun emplacements and blockhouses had been planned and intended as part of a fixed line method of defence, to provide static and rigid defences beyond which an attacker could not pass. As the British were managing to overcome the problem by developing new ways of countering their presence, the Germans were changing their methods to elastic defences — the use of strong outposts in a weakly-held zone, which would break up and delay an attack while infantry fell back and then counterattacked a reduced and stretched force. This new strategy had begun in a small way during the Arras battles and was expanded to defend against the expected attack on Messines Ridge. It evolved during the fighting in August to October, 1917, into an effective method; the pill boxes and bunkers on which the Germans had expended so much trouble were found to be easily incorporated into the new tactics. By this time the British hierarchy had officially acknowledged that pill boxes could hold up an attack, and recommended that smoke grenades and Stokes mortar bombs be used to blind machine-gun emplacements.

The elastic or 'defence in depth' policy also found favour with the British, who, when developing their own defences in anticipation of a German offensive the following spring, devised

Concrete bunkers could be constructed and disguised to look like houses, barns, and so on. Windows, nailed or painted on, and a wickerwork roof could look quite authentic.

the forward zone, battle zone and rear zone. The British faced the same problems in constructing the strongpoints as had the Germans: the problems of building structures, often close to the front line or under observation from the air, without disclosing the presence and nature of the work. Both before and after completion it was necessary to hide the structure.

Wherever a pill box, bunker, dug-out or observation post was sited, camouflage was essential for protection from land and air observation. A number of methods were employed: adapting an existing building or natural feature such as a mound or hillock; imitating a building or structure; or simply blending into whatever natural or defensive features existed in the area.

A common method, especially for low or trench-level constructions, was to cover the structure with earth, turf, brushwood or rubble to match the immediate surroundings. This was generally effective, although not always permanent, as constant shelling shook or blew off the loose covering, revealing the clearly visible, relatively white, fresh concrete underneath. It was frequently necessary to replace the coverings to maintain the camouflage. In the Ypres Salient following heavy shelling the

German defenders sometimes re-covered their pill boxes with mud each night, making them very difficult for the British infantry and artillery observers to identify.

In shell-torn ground the lack of features made the positioning of a suspected pill box very problematic, and precise map references for the artillery or infantry attacks were difficult to pinpoint. An example of this was reported by the 6th London Regiment, part of the 58th Division, attacking Hubner Farm from St Julien. After several assaults on 6 and 7 September, 1918, against a particular pill box (MEBU), the map reference was finally determined within a range of 50 yards, and reported to brigade headquarters. It was also reported that:

(a) the pill box was much nearer than they were told it would be, and

(b) there was a slope or bank in front of the MEBU which may have been the breastwork.

Only two MEBUs were seen definitely, the second 25 to 30 yards south of the one already mentioned.

The MEBU attacked was about ten feet square, but reliability cannot be attached to this statement as opinions differ.

The attackers were unable to identify whether the pill box was in front of or behind the main Hubner Trench. A sketch of the position accompanied the report, suggesting the pill box was probably in the continuation of Hubner Trench running north-west. The location of adjacent pill boxes was given as 'probable'; some were 'probably occupied'.

In a featureless landscape it was difficult to identify which particular pill box was which, and therefore which one a particular unit should attack. During an attack machine-gun fire was frequently found to be directed from unsuspected emplacements. Following the assaults by the 6th London Regiment, the Queen Victoria's Rifles, also part of the 58th Division, were ordered to attack a concrete emplacement near Springfield, 200 yards further along Hubner Trench, on 8 September, 1917. The attack failed, with many casualties, due to incorrect information. The brigade headquarters reported that:

As this concrete emplacement was non-existent, and as they were being shot into in the back from concrete

Brushwood fascines were used to provide both formwork and camouflage, although even with an earth-covered roof the camouflage was not always fully effective. This one south of Passchendaele village would be given away by its silhouette.

emplacements on both flanks, it appeared that the position would be untenable in the daylight. A withdrawal was therefore ordered.

To ensure effective camouflage it was essential to provide screening for the preparatory work, as excavation of deep holes, removal of spoil and the presence of a work-force could be seen from the air. The conversion of existing buildings with minimal exterior changes was the easiest and most effective method of constructing a strongpoint, as exterior brick walls and roofs had the advantage of providing formwork for concrete. With groups of houses or farm buildings, one or two could be turned into bomb-proof shelters, with existing exterior damage helping to blend them into their surroundings. Another advantage was that the outer part of the building would act as a burster layer, setting off a shell's fuse. In Flanders much use was made of this method of camouflage for pill boxes and bunkers, especially by the Germans.

Where buildings did not exist and above-ground construction

was needed, a new 'house' or 'barn' would be built. Whilst not practicable in the front line, where changes of scenery were noticeable, this was effective in the rear areas. Using local architecture, and with painted or affixed features such as windows, solid bunkers could be made unobtrusive and well concealed.

False tiled or thatched roofs completed the disguise. Closer to the front, other methods of camouflage were required. Breastworks and trench lines, rows of bushes or trees (if any), and folds in the ground offered opportunities for concealment. A breastwork of sandbags or fascines could be used both for temporary concealment or longer-term camouflage. The concrete texture offered by sacking or brushwood, particularly when covered by mud, made identification from a distance difficult. If a bunker or pill box was constructed in the open, fascines, brushwood and earth coverings were used to conceal the concrete. Such camouflage was either laid loosely over the structure or held down by ropes or wire netting.

Whilst the body and exterior of the bunker or pill box were the important factors in providing protection for the inhabitants, the latter had to function and operate inside the structure. Improving the internal conditions thus became a major consideration.

Drainage was a problem, particularly in subterranean constructions, and many designs included a sump to trap water which could be pumped out.

Acceptable air was another problem, especially in pill boxes, as air for breathing had to be allowed in, whilst gas fumes had to be kept out, and both sides developed gas-proof curtains for doorways and other openings.

Gases from machine-gun fire were a problem in pill boxes and had to be expelled, either by ventilation through the roof or through the embrasure. Later in the war the British developed a parabolic cup for the ends of the machine-gun muzzle which projected the gases forward.

Heating and lighting were important operations in command posts, communications centres and hospitals. White interior walls helped candles and electric bulbs to brighten the interior, as did rear-facing 'window' openings admitting natural light. Domestic materials, decorations and furniture ('borrowed' from empty houses and stores) added to the aesthetic appeal and comfort for the inhabitants. Heat, when it could be provided, contributed to these home comforts; many shelters and bunkers, particularly in rear areas, had stoves and chimney vents added during construction.

Nevertheless, heat, light, comfort and decoration aside, the real test was the structure's ability to withstand shell fire. Other major considerations were its effectiveness in preventing attacking infantry from moving directly towards or around it, and its ability to defend or contribute to the defence of any other structures with which it was grouped.

The method by which a pill box defended itself and its neighbours depended on its basic style as well as its siting and positioning. Certain factors determined its potential in meeting the demands made on it: whether it contained gun-ports or embrasures from which to direct fire, enabling the garrison to fire on demand; or whether it was 'blind' − a structure in which the gun crew sheltered, only to emerge and fire from around or over it when required. Those fitted with gun-ports allowed permanent observation over the surrounding ground, and fire could be maintained at all times while the troops themselves were under protection. This type proved difficult to capture. Both types had advantages and disadvantages, but both accounted for a very large number of casualties on both sides.

Experience gained at Vimy and Bullecourt during the Arras battles was exploited by the British during the third battle of Ypres with varying degrees of success. An early tactic, which proved to be wasteful of lives, involved rushing pill boxes with enough infantrymen to ensure that some of them got close enough to be effective in the attack.

Assaults proved more successful when troops covered each other with volleys of rifle, trench mortar and rifle-grenade fire. The Mills No. 23 rifle-grenade, if fired from within eighty yards, was found to be very effective. Rifle-grenades fired into gun-ports caused havoc within the pill box; rifle volleys helped to distract and hold down the defenders whilst the attackers closed in. Closing in and outflanking was helped if the ground around contained hollows or shell-holes, and smoke bombs were used to mar the vision of the occupants and screen the attackers. A more common tactic was for Lewis gunners to engage the occupants whilst troops worked their way round the back of the pill box to rush the rear entry, the practicalities of which depended upon ground conditions and the locations of adjacent pill boxes.

Numerous acts of bravery, often single-handed, were recorded in attacks on pill boxes, such as dropping grenades and phosphorous bombs or firing revolvers at the crew inside through the gun-slits. In one instance, Sergeant Grimbaldeston of the King's Own Scottish Borderers and Private Hancock of the Worcestershire Regiment threatened a pill box's inhabitants into surrender. Many Victoria Crosses were won in the taking of pill boxes.

'Blind' constructions were designed to be used in a different manner from those with gun-ports, and therefore different methods of attack were required. These shelters were intended only to provide shell-cover to guns and crew. A successful attack was dependent upon getting close to the shelter before the emerging crew could set up their guns and prepare themselves for action. Success in this endeavour varied. With good conditions and accurate timing the infantry could reach the shelter before the enemy garrison emerged, making capture fairly easy. But imprecise timing, poor ground conditions or the accuracy of an enemy barrage often resulted in many causalities as the attacking infantry were caught on their way to the pill box by machine-gun or rifle fire.

Another factor, of course, was the fighting spirit of the defenders and attackers. This varied enormously: many pill boxes and shelters were tenaciously defended, while the dispirited and demoralized defenders of others emerged without a struggle.

The timing of a major attack or the need to keep up with a barrage often meant that pill boxes were by-passed, leaving their inhabitants free either to attack the second assault wave or fire into the back of those who had passed. Several instances were recorded of the enemy emerging after the first or second attacking wave had passed, and it became necessary to appoint 'moppers-up' whose task was to ensure that by-passed strongpoints were fully taken and cleared. Experience demanded that a captured pill box be immediately consolidated and prepared to resist counterattacks, as the enemy would use similar tactics to recapture their former dwellings from their new occupants.

Shelters were constructed with the purpose of allowing troops to sit safely through a barrage, ready to emerge and fight as soon as the shelling stopped.

At various stages of the First World War there was much discussion on the relative merits of defence in depth (which came to be adopted by both sides in various forms), and the holding of one or more defence lines. After the third battle of Ypres in 1917, the Germans investigated the efficiency of dug-outs and pill boxes. Mined, or very deep, dug-outs were found in many instances to be death-traps and were not encouraged. A German document of 3 September, 1917, ordering the construction of defensive positions around Ypres for the coming winter, advised:

> The group regards machine-gun emplacements, when strongly constructed and suitably sited, as the most essential requisite for the defence of the whole position when fighting is resumed. Concrete structures, which should at the same time all be constructed for use as machine-gun emplacements, must be of low profile, and the slopes of the earth covering them must be kept flat. The construction of shelters and dug-outs must be carried out at the same time throughout the whole defensive zone. The construction of machine-gun

The same scene today.

Concealment from aerial observation could sometimes be achieved fairly easily. Haus Kathe, just outside Polygon Wood, shows how a few roof timbers could be very effective. The use of body armour for sentries looking over the top illustrates how watch was kept.

emplacements in the ground between the trenches must
be taken in hand at once on a particularly liberal scale.[15]

During a bombardment, or simply when hit by a stray shell, the strength and integrity of the structure was of prime importance to those sheltering inside. Erich Maria Remarque was assigned to the 2nd Company of the Field Recruiting Depot, Guards Reserve Division, in front of Arras before he was transferred to Flanders.[16] Sheltering from a prolonged bombardment, he describes how the concrete-block shelter was able to withstand a direct hit, although cracking along all joints and filling with sulphur fumes. Remarque was thankful that he and his comrades were not in one of the lighter, more recent dug-outs, in which they would not have survived.

The British were also glad of the concrete protection provided by captured German strongpoints when it was their turn to shelter. John Tucker describes his gratitude to the Germans for their strong concrete work while sheltering from German shell fire in a pill box on the Menin Road at Ypres near Inverness

Copse.[17] The pill box, which the British had not been able to destroy when it was in German hands, had withstood both British and German shell hits. Similar praise was given by Gladden, occupying a German front-line shelter in Canada Trench near Wieltje. Its thick concrete walls were sufficiently strong to withstand direct hits, including one over a weak spot, the door, which was facing the Germans:

> The dug-out's survival from such a tremendous blow
> at its weakest spot was in itself a great tribute to the
> German engineers.[18]

Edwin Vaughan sat in the Boiler House, a concrete bunker on the outskirts of St Julien, watching it disintegrate during repeated hits by German shells. A huge block of concrete over his commanding officer's head moved half an inch inwards with every shell-burst, and Vaughan thought it was only a matter of time before the pill box would collapse.[19]

Both British and Germans constructed bunkers and pill boxes where needed, in and behind the front line. When the line moved, the side gaining ground sometimes inherited intact and usable bunkers. These were welcomed by the front-line troops, providing them with the cover previously enjoyed by their opponents. The main problem with occupying such a bunker was that it faced the wrong direction, with the doorway open to the enemy and inviting his attention — which he gladly, frequently and deliberately gave. The newly occupied bunker had to be 'turned around' by blocking up the doorway and adding a new one in the rear (a problem not often experienced by the Germans, who lost so many pill boxes but won so few). In addition to this 'turning round', the Allies took it upon themselves to finish abandoned and partially-completed structures.

Fighting in the Ypres Salient in 1917 left many bunkers in British hands. Often in full view of the enemy, they provided much-needed cover for the troops. The thickness of the concrete and the steel reinforcement in the front walls gave many Royal Engineers companies trying to create new doorways an awkward problem to solve, however, as merely being seen working on a bunker could invite shells from the enemy.

Conversion work was sometimes a reasonably easy task: the 427th Field Company adapted several German bunkers by simply

Pilkem Ridge signalling station, sometimes known as the Viking Ship because of its shape. Constructed by the German Marine Corps under engineer Ziegler, using reinforcing steel rods taken from a commandeered engineering workshop, the very thick walls on the side facing the Allies required their skilled use of explosives to produce a doorway safe from German observers. Captured by the French in July, 1917, it was turned around by 554 (Dundee) Royal Engineers.

concreting steel joists over and in front of the structure, creating another roof and wall and acting as a burster layer. Other companies preferred to cut a new doorway in the front wall, but 135 Company Royal Engineers had difficulty in providing the right tools to their sections on the Pilkem Ridge, 'the concrete being very hard and breaking points of tools'.

Steel reinforcement was always a problem but 235 Company Royal Engineers, likewise working on the Pilkem Ridge, was fortunate enough to have an oxyacetylene cutter. Explosives were used, with variable results. A technique perfected by 554 (Dundee) Royal Engineers Company was a jump-hole of between two and three inches diameter, fifteen inches deep, at an angle of sixty degrees to the horizontal, tamped with a charge of between four and six ounces of ammonal, depending on wall thickness. A three-foot diameter hole appeared when the charge was set off, two of which made a gap suitable for trimming and tidying up into a convenient doorway. A good example of this handiwork can be seen in the front wall of a large signalling station on the Pilkem Ridge, in what was Wood 16.

Whether or not a new entrance was needed, the doorway facing the enemy had to be blocked as protection from shells and snipers' bullets. Techniques varied from concreting-in the doorway and windows, if any, to rebuilding and providing machine-gun or observation ports. Several examples of 'turn arounds' can be seen in the Ypres area. Majors Farm on the Pilkem Ridge, the work of 256 Company Royal Engineers, shows a German bunker with a rear door cut in, a new front section with an observation post, and a concreted-in doorway. Nearby at Gourmier Farm is an example of new walls attached to protect the rear doorway.

In the area taken in the Messines offensive, many pill boxes and bunkers were adapted to troop defences and accommodation. Australians holding this sector in the winter of 1917-1918 were active in 'turning around', repairing damage and completing

Majors Farm pill box, Pilkem Ridge. After being captured to ensure consolidation of the ridge during the winter 1917-1918, that part of the bunker to the left (darker coloured concrete) needed turning around. This meant creating a new doorway in the rear wall, with the original doorway allowing access to the new section now facing the Germans. Many similar alterations were carried out by 256 and other Royal Engineers companies.

The Australians holding White Château at the end of the Dammstrasse adapted a damaged German concrete-block pill box so that the doorway and strongest wall both faced the correct directions.

bunkers left unfinished by the enemy. A concrete-block pill box by White Château at the end of the Dammstrasse is a good example of work by the 1st Australian Division, who dismantled the original and rebuilt it as a small shelter. The majority of solid concrete bunkers were adapted using the 'cut or blow a hole in the wall' technique for a door, concreting-in the original door, and strengthening the rear wall.

14 *Official History of Australia in the War,* Vol.IV, by C. E. W. Bean.
15 *On the construction of positions on the Ypres Battle Front for the coming winter* issued by Gruppe Wytschaete. The document was translated and distributed by the School of Military Engineering and General Staff Intelligence in October 1917.
16 *Im Westen nichts Neues (All Quiet on the Western Front)* by Erich Maria Remarque. Christened Erich Paul Remark and training with Reserve Battalion IR 78, he changed his name in 1923.
17 *Johnny Get Your Gun* by John F. Tucker (William Kimber Ltd., London 1978).
18 *Ypres 1917* by Norman Gladden (William Kimber Ltd., London 1967).
19 *Some Desperate Glory* by Edwin Campion Vaughan (Leo Cooper, London 1981).

CHAPTER SIX

Defence Lines

While the British army sat out the winter of 1916 licking its wounds in wet trenches and dug-outs after the battle of the Somme, and planning further major strides forward in the coming spring, the Germans themselves had been busy. In taking their beating they had learned some valuable lessons on defensive cover, and this knowledge would be put to good use in their planning of a strategic withdrawal.

The Hindenburg Line was designed both to shorten their front, enabling a better use of resources, and to site their defences in positions most favourable to them. Using a spur or switch (their Wotan Line) covering the northern flank, the line made use of the geography south-eastward from Arras, on past St Quentin and to the west of Laon. This was the central section of a line eventually intended to reach from the Belgian coast to the Swiss border.

The main, second and reserve lines were designed to make use of all hills and slopes, with much open ground in front in which an attacking force would find little cover. Dense lines of barbed wire were positioned to channel attackers into places which were covered by concrete-covered machine-gun emplacements.

Once the strategists and planners had done their work, the engineers and pioneers had from mid-November to early March to complete the job. The manpower requirements for such a scheme were very high. The workforce was made up of the military, civilian workers from Germany, conscripted Belgians and large numbers of prisoners of war, mainly Russians. Hundreds of kilometres of trench-works, up to four metres wide to prevent tanks passing, together with mined dug-outs and shelters had to be prepared.

To provide shelter from shell fire and bombs much use was made of concrete. MEBUs, such as the *Panzermebu* (Panzer, or armoured, MEBUs were concrete bunkers incorporating steel

The Hindenburg defence system included above ground and sunken pill boxes. This example in Joncourt, has resisted later attempts at removal.

Very large tonnages of concrete-making materials were used, requiring large-volume concrete mixers and large construction crews.

plates), were designed to provide cover for observers, accommodation for defenders and shelter for machine-gun crews. The MEBUs, or pill boxes, were connected to the trench and dug-out system, giving mutually covering observation and firepower.

While some earlier German concrete constructions were hurriedly made in dangerous circumstances, those in the Hindenburg Line were well thought-out designs built under almost ideal conditions. The British were several miles away, so attention could be given to sound excavation and foundations, exact positioning of steel reinforcement, and correct mixing and placing of concrete. Large tonnages of cement, steel and aggregate had to be produced, transported and placed, and pioneer parks were set up on sites fed by canals and railways for the distribution of these materials. These parks also did much work producing timber formwork and bending reinforcing steel.

Information on the siting and construction of large defence works in the enemy rear area was supplied to British intelligence as early as late October, 1916. Royal Flying Corps patrols reported earthworks near Quéant to the south-east of Arras, while further reports in November of that year supplied information on a new defence line around Bullecourt. Adding to this intelligence, an escaped Russian prisoner stated that many of his ex-colleagues still in German hands were constructing concrete dug-outs. Other sources provided similar indications, although at the time no special importance was given to this pooled information.

In late February British troops noticed that the German lines appeared to be quieter than usual, and consequent patrolling along several sectors found the trenches empty. On 24 February, 1917, the 22nd Manchesters and the South Staffords found the village of Serre empty of the enemy. On the same day V Corps signalled to the divisions in its sector:

> Indications point to the enemy having retired along the
> whole front of the V Corps, and touch has been lost.
> Touch with the enemy will be obtained tonight.

The search to find the Germans was on, and the Third Army reported on 14 March, 1917:

> The German divisions facing the Fifth Army have
> withdrawn their front to Bapaume, Bucquoy, Monchy.

The Corps in the Third Army were then given orders to follow the Germans to the Hindenburg Line.

It was some time before British intelligence were able to get sufficient information on the siting, intended method of use and strengths of the system. In August, 1917, after several attacks had been made upon the Hindenburg Line, a report was produced.[21] This advised that both front and support trenches were generally on reverse slopes, which gave direct artillery observation from heights in the rear, and any attack on the line would be over ground under observation. Shell-proof concrete signalling stations, facing towards the rear, were included. As if this was not enough, artillery observation by the attacker was denied.

The support trenches were between 200 and 300 yards from the front trench, with wide belts of barbed wire (some believed to be electrified) so erected as to channel attacking infantry toward the machine-guns. These machine-guns were not placed at the angles of the wire belts where they were expected and assumed to be. Also, many 'blind' ferro-concrete dug-outs had been constructed to provide shell-proof accommodation without machine-gun or rifle embrasures or ports.

The report went on:

> No concrete or covered M.G. emplacements have been found. Concrete emplacements have, however, been reported in the support trench and between the support and front trenches in canal banks and in hillocks, woods, etc.

In contradiction, it also indicated that in some areas concrete shelters were numerous:

> Where possible, however, concrete shelters have been made every 50 to 100 yards for the garrison of the front line.

Some parts of the line were attacked during the battle of Arras in April and May of 1917, soon after the German retreat in the spring. This falling-back and pursuit was a new type of fighting — open warfare. Trench warfare was soon to become the norm again, but a new German ingredient became evident in the use of large numbers of concrete machine-gun emplacements. The pill-box era had arrived.

Following the capture of the villages of Holnon, Savy and

In many sectors of the line existing buildings were used for camouflage. Each of these houses near Lens is a concrete gun emplacement, firing through the window. (Imperial War Museum CO 1879)

Canadians examining a bunker, showing the 'window'. (Imperial War Museum CO 1878)

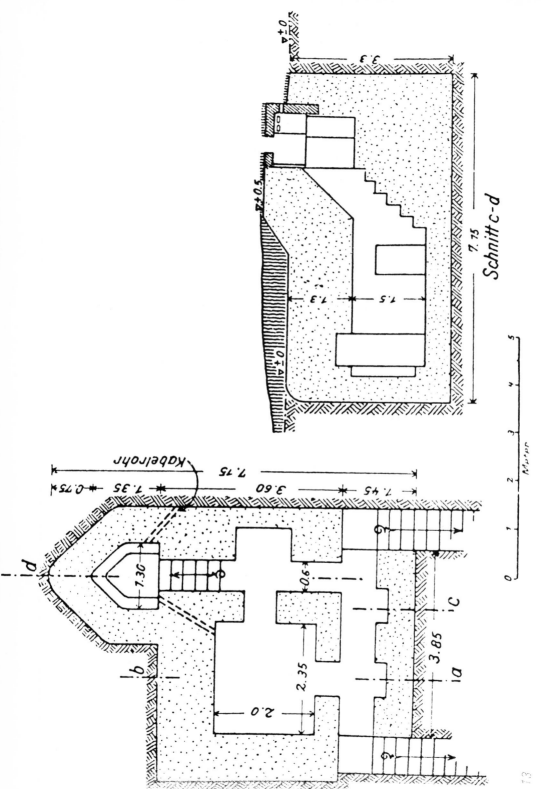

Schnitt c-d

Kabelrohr

With siting and layout carefully chosen, even observation posts could at ground level – six to nine inches – give both observation and shelter to the defenders.

13

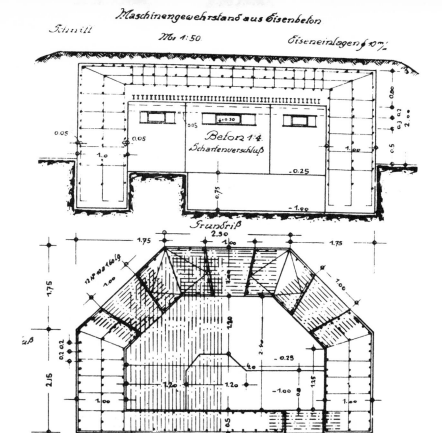

Various standard patterns were used in different sectors. This one was widely used, and influenced British pill box design in both 1918 and 1940.

Selency opposite St Quentin, and Ronssoy and Lempire further north, the Australians took Doignies, Louverval and Noreil. In the latter they found a large concrete gun emplacement built into a house. Other villages fell, such as Croisilles and Hénin, and by 9 April the enemy, except in a few isolated outposts, were safely ensconced behind the concrete and wire of the Hindenburg Line. But on the day the Germans were settling into their new quarters in the southern half of the line, their colleagues in the northern sector were under attack.

On 9 April, 1917, the British attacked the line between Hermies and Tilloy-les-Mofflaines in front of Arras and Vimy Ridge. The Germans had planned a concentration of concrete shelters on and around the ridge, but labour and material shortages had been

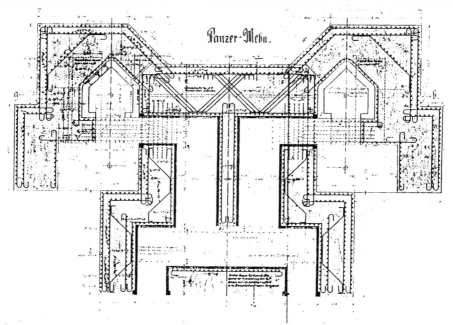

Panzer-Mebu.

90

German 'standard' designs varied between army groups, and several patterns were used along the Siegfried Stellung or Hindenburg Line. The sector between Heninel and Bullecourt was strongly defended and incorporated many pill boxes and bunkers of variations on one design. The design gave shell-proof protection, strong steel observation

hatches, and a ledge or firing-step for the machine-gun crew to fire over the roof at attacking troops. This plan illustrates the complexity of design and complicated construction, while the photo series shows the Panzermebu or pill box at various stages of construction, the same pill box today (lower right), and the inclusion of a steel observation hatch which was concreted in. A variation on the design allowed for a single artillery observer. The British troops who captured lengths of this line envied the Germans for having such protection during the artillery battles, and later used the shelters themselves whenever possible. B Company of the Royal West Surrey Regiment adopted this one near Bullecourt for their headquarters (top); other troops made themselves at home in others (below).

diverted to construction of the line to the south, and the wintry weather which reportedly 'prevented concrete from setting' left the Vimy Ridge defences thinner than the Germans wanted. The old front line and rear defences in front of Arras fell fairly easily, but the Allied advance stopped in front of Rouex, Fontaine-le-Croisilles and other well-defended villages.

The attack by the Anzacs and the British 62nd Division on that part of the line running through the village of Bullecourt was unsuccessful, as the new concrete pill boxes proved too tough to crack. This failure was followed by another when, eighteen days later on 3 May, the Anzacs, again with the 62nd Division, tried again. The 7th Division joined in the fracas and for the next two weeks the village was bitterly contested. A major cause of this lack of progress, bringing with it severe casualties, was the enemy's skilful use of concreted machine-gun emplacements or MEBUs, referred to in various of the 7th Division's reports as Mebis, Magus, Mimbus, Mebi and Mebontes. Bullecourt eventually fell as the line moved forward slightly, and many of these pill boxes were used as accommodation, company and signal headquarters, and aid posts. Those used through the summer and winter were all given names for location identification – Og, Gog, Magog, Neptune, Pluto, Jove, Mars, Vulcan, Argus and Mercury. These godly names suggest the respect felt for the inanimate concrete monoliths.

Through the autumn and winter of 1917 the Germans sat watching the British on the lower ground in this part of the line, only emerging to attack them in the 1918 spring offensive. Their line of concrete constructions had fulfilled its role. They used the line again when they were driven back later in 1918, but this time their defence organization was not nearly as thorough. Using the old British front line as an outer defence, they dug in and awaited the expected onslaught. In late September and early October it came. Heavy British bombardment destroyed most of the pill boxes and bunkers, and the line was taken.

The construction of defensive lines, trenches, bunkers, pill boxes and observation points was not new to the Germans. They already had experience in the planning, supply of labour and materials, and operational aspects. Although they enjoyed a good relationship with the Dutch and, as covered earlier, made much

Along the Belgian border with The Netherlands, the Germans built solid defences incorporating concrete bunkers and pill boxes, often disguised as houses and barns. This strongpoint contained a heavy shell-proof bunker and support for anti-aircraft fire. The constructions, minus camouflage, can still be seen (inset).

use of it to further their end, they had always considered the possibility of a British attack from the rear: through The Netherlands, with or without the help of the Dutch. In 1916 they had built a defence line along the Belgian/Dutch border to repel any such attack. Level trenches were impractical due to the low-lying, flat land and its proximity to the sea, so the line took the form of numerous strongpoints incorporating the dykes along the border. These dykes provided perfect cover for bunkers, while giving some protection from shell fire. Trenches with wiring in front were cut in, forming a strong defence line. Command posts were built behind this line, camouflaged to imitate houses and barns. Manned by skeleton crews, this line of strongpoints was never used and saw no service other than border-watching and preventing civilians escaping from occupied Belgium.

By early 1918, it was clear to the British that the situation was about to change. The Germans were expected to launch a major offensive in an attempt to take the Channel ports. Up until then British concrete work for pill boxes and bunkers had been partly left to localized initiative. Cement, steel and stone had not always been made available in the required quantites, lip-service had been paid to solidly constructed protection, and such defences had always been considered temporary. In many sectors, though, the army had been active in building concrete defences, and many thoughts, ideas, methods and concepts of concrete protection and

Many bunkers were built into dykes, with adjacent trench lines to cover the border, both for defence against a possible British invasion through Holland and to prevent Belgians civilians from escaping.

cover were circulating. Several attempts were made to pool all this experience to give the best available advice to engineers and tacticians.

In February, 1918, the British engineer-in-chief published his *Use of Ferro-Concrete in Dug-out Construction* (see Appendix 3). This document covered all aspects of concealment and protection for dug-outs, machine-gun emplacements, observation posts, and so on, advising that concealment from observation and protection from shell fire were fundamentally antagonistic. It discussed when to sacrifice full protection for concealment (in observation posts and certain machine-gun positions), and when full protection was the major consideration, even at the expense of perfect concealment (in garrison dug-outs, for example).

The disadvantages of solid concrete against ferro-concrete (concrete reinforced with steel) were stated. Accepting the proven value of reinforced concrete in the construction of dug-outs, the document stressed that they could be greatly weakened by poor design and construction, by the type of reinforcement and its location in the concrete (at inside and external faces), and by methods of binding and tying. It detailed the minimum practical concrete thickness, and the relative values of thickness for different materials and protection against different types of shell. All this, together with French research findings, was tabulated. The report included drawings showing reinforced concrete machine-gun emplacements and shelters to illustrate the general principles.

When the line around Ypres was shortened many bunkers and pill boxes in the area given up by the Germans were destroyed, although those on the Pilkem Ridge were retained. The destroying of such constructions was not without danger: a Major Shaw, MC, of the Royal Engineers was killed while demolishing a pill box at Mill Cot near Potijze.

In the south, Australian engineers were busy strengthening existing bunkers and building new ones on the Messines Ridge. By the end of March, 1918, they had repaired, constructed or were in the process of building seventy-two pill boxes in addition to dug-outs and shelters, many for accommodation rather than defence. Their records highlight tremendous thoroughness and professionalism in construction, from the erection of camouflage, through work in progress and the precision bending, lapping and

In the winter of 1917-1918 the Australians renovated many pill boxes and bunkers on Messines Ridge. This one near Wyteschaete is nearing completion in March, 1918, as part of preparations for the expected German offensive. (Imperial War Museum E (Aus) 2346)

detailing of reinforcement, to the mixing and placing of concrete. In all cases a detailed specification was produced and used. The New Zealanders were also busy effecting high quality work − one of their shell-proof bunkers near Messines took a direct hit from a heavy shell and, although suffering some external damage, took the strain.

Further south, other works were in progress. From late 1917 pill boxes were constructed at Ploegsteert Wood, with bunkers being built behind the lines around the village itself. At Fleurbaix, in front of the River Lys, eleven were designed as half-subterranean, with flat roofs, walls pitched at a 45 degree angle and a blast wall protecting the doorways. A concrete field hospital was included in the complex, at the time garrisoned by the 40th Battalion Machine Gun Corps. 229 Field Company Royal Engineers were working on these when they and the 40th Division were forced to retire on 9 April, 1918.

Royal Engineers attached to the 42nd Division spent a very busy winter concreting defences around the La Bassée canal sector. 427, 428 and 429 Field Companies had some experience in concreting from their efforts around Nieuport in October, 1917. Now they started concrete work in earnest on both sides of the canal. Many bunkers and pill boxes were constructed in the front and reserve lines, demanding vast quantities of cement and aggregate. This was shipped in by barge to a Royal Engineers dump at Gorre, then taken forward at night in sandbags to the point of use. The scale of operations can be estimated from the specifications and material required for one pill box, No. 4, built

A typical British bunker built at Wimbledon − the Gravenstafel crossroads − just out of the sight of the Germans in Passchendaele.

'BLACK BUTT' DUGOUT.

SECTION

Shell-proof shelters produced by laying a thick layer of concrete (usually reinforced with either steel bars or expanded steel mesh) over an elephant-iron inner lining were relatively simple and easy to construct, especially where the supply of timber for formwork was limited. Depending upon the quality and thickness of concrete and its reinforcement, protection from all but a heavy shell could be provided. The curved roof helped to reduce the effects of a hit from some angles. An added benefit was the steel lining, which helped prevent concrete splintering on the inside when hit. The curved shelter became a fairly standard design for the British; early designs for 'shrapnel/splinter-proof' shelters (with earth or filled sandbags over the steel lining) evolved into the concrete-covered shell-proof

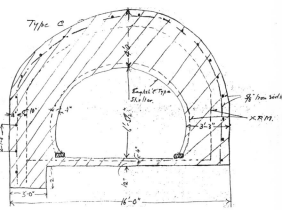

models. Further protection could be provided by laying earth or sandbags over the concrete as a concussion layer, then a thin concrete burster layer over this to detonate the fuse. The drawing section (opposite top left) shows the design; beside it is the result today. Designs varied within divisions, with Royal Engineers incorporating their own ideas (top right). A number of design variations can still be found today along the Western Front, as in this shelter (bottom) near Dickebusch, which had one doorway blocked to form a machine-gun embrasure when the Germans came closer in 1918. The Germans also found the basic design simple to construct and camouflage (opposite lower left), although few 'standard' German designs for concreted elephant-steel shelters were produced. Those constructed were the result of front line or forward conditions. The design of those captured (opposite lower right) certainly influenced the British, who were to adopt these ideas.

in the Marylebone Road Trench facing the Cuinchy Brickstacks off the La Bassée Road:

Internal dimensions 10'4" x 4'9" x 5'3"
1,907 full sandbags of shingle
953 bags sand
476 bags cement

This meant a total of 3,336 bags, each weighing sixty pounds, being carried over a mile of frosty duckboard tracks at night.

Many such pill boxes and bunkers were constructed: elephant-steel shelters with four-feet thick reinforced concrete facing the enemy and a solid cast-concrete dome over the top. In many cases expanded metal was cast into inner and outer faces. These were no doubt welcomed by the 55th Division, who held up the Germans at this point after taking over the line from the 42nd Division.

Further south towards St Quentin, odd batches of pill boxes were constructed at random, the number and siting being left to the personal preference of the divisional or brigade commander and staff.

General Gough, commanding the Fifth Army holding the southernmost sector of the British line, was convinced that the enemy would be attacking in force in this sector, and that the defences as they stood would be insufficient to repel or hold such an attack. He demanded that they be strengthened and deepened.

During 1917 the policy of the British Army had been entirely offensive, and all its resources in engineers, material, etc. had been devoted to dealing with this side of the operations. Defensive measures, therefore, had been much neglected.[21]

Moreover he discovered that, to the east of Villers Bretonneux, French farm workers were busy dismantling defences to recultivate the land, and these particular defences, built two years earlier, were very likely to be needed again. Following much correspondence with General Headquarters, the workforce on the Fifth Army defences was greatly enlarged. Supplies of engineering materials were increased, and Indian, Italian and Chinese labourers and prisoners of war were employed to augment the British. But General Gough remained dissatisfied with the rate of progress, saying the front line and battle zone:

were quite incomplete, with very few if any shell-proof
dug-outs in them for machine-gun detachments, brigade
or battalion headquarters, dressing stations, etc.

Following the German attack in March and April, 1918, the line
stabilized and the British began frantically constructing various
strong defences. The lessons learned from the German use of
concrete pill boxes had at last had their effect, and with the
knowledge that large numbers of enemy troops released from
their duties in the east were joining their comrades in the west,
suitable defence lines needed to be prepared. From north of
Ypres, where the British line joined the Belgian army, to Moreil
south of Villers Bretonneux where it met that of the French First
Army, strongly defended front, support and reserve lines were
constructed with reinforced concrete and official blessing.

Stock was taken of the current position in respect of designs,
production, use and siting of pill boxes. As mentioned earlier, in
September, 1917, Royal Engineers attached to the British First
Army had started building a factory at Aire-sur-la-Lys to produce
block-built pill boxes. The scheme was accelerated and production
capacity increased, with a School of Concrete opened to give
instruction to the officers and men who were to install them. The
idea was taken up by the Second Army, which then produced kits
at Arques. These, together with the Moir pill boxes from
Richborough and the Australian-designed Hobbs pill boxes,
meant that the British army was well supplied with pre-cast pill
boxes and bunkers in 1918.

In addition, supplies of materials were made available for *in
situ* concrete works. Many companies of Royal Engineers had
experience in repairing and building concrete pill boxes and
bunkers, and it was thought prudent to pool this knowledge and
the various disciplines relevant to the design, construction and
use of concrete. An inspector of concrete defences was attached
to the staff at GHQ. His duties were to:

    a) Inspect the work of army companies as regards
    technical matters in erection, transport, rate of progress
    and methods of execution;
    b) Report on proposed improvements in designs;
    c) Record all experiments and known effects of shell fire;
    d) Liaise with concrete factories and armies as regards

manufacture and needs respectively; and

e) Maintain and disseminate knowledge of new patterns
for trial and manufacture.

In addition to this a specialist Royal Engineers company was attached to each army to advise on concrete construction. Companies 220, 221, 222, 223 and 224 of the Royal Engineers were attached to the Second, Fifth, Third, First and Fourth Armies respectively. Each consisted of five officers and 257 other ranks, plus mechanical transport. Supplies of materials were made more available for field companies (aggregate had always been in good supply but roadworks had taken priority over other uses), and large amounts of cement were imported from England. Even though most concrete was supplied pre-cast, in February, 1917, 30,000 barrels of cement had been supplied, used largely for mix-in-place concrete and mortar, and tonnages were increased further in 1918.

Cement was transported in sacks of 244 pounds each and in barrels of 422 and 330 pounds. Most was supplied in barrels, as sacks allowed damp to penetrate and set the cement. The troops also preferred barrels, as the wood from them had other uses. The Associated Portland Cement Company, the main suppliers, complained that many barrels were not returned and those which were had been opened the wrong end or otherwise damaged.

The French thought it unnecessary for the British to import cement into Dunkirk, Calais and Boulogne at a time when France was producing 15,000 to 20,000 tonnes of cement per month in the Boulogne area, but experiencing great difficulty in transporting it to its sectors in central France. They suggested that the British use French cement from Boulogne whilst delivering British cement to Nantes or St Nazaire. The British did not accept this kind offer, nor a similar one made later.

With their backs to the wall, and the Channel ports under threat, the British devoted themselves to constructing defence lines, although more were planned than actually constructed, due to a lack of labour. Ypres was considered to be worth defending, so several Royal Engineers companies worked in the front line and the École Switch Line just in front of the ramparts at Ypres. Just to their rear, 228 Field Company constructed concrete bunkers and 208 Company placed Moir pill boxes on the town ramparts.

Two of these are still there, looking out over the southern approach to the town. Behind and flanking the town the construction embraced the support line at Brielen and Vlamertinghe, with a reserve line behind this.

Whilst infantry, machine-gun and engineering companies were stating and exhibiting their faith in concrete pill boxes and bunkers for the defence line, some in higher authority were not convinced. On 8 June, 1918, Second Army staff suggested the construction of tunnelled brigade and battalion headquarters and shelters for troops, and requests for test borings were made accordingly. The lieutenant-general commanding II Corps, which was busy constructing the lines, felt concrete constructions to be much preferable to tunnelled dug-outs, and wrote to his superiors on 13 June:

> 1. Experience gained by the II Corps in the construction and ultimate value of tunnelled dug-outs in Flanders has, I think, conclusively shown that they do not warrant the time, labour or material expended on them.
>
> 2. [Details of failures and problems with tunnelled dug-outs.]
>
> 3. On the other hand the construction of concrete pill boxes has in every way proved a success.
>
> 4. I hope therefore that, if skilled labour is available, a proportion may be allotted to the II Corps for the construction of concrete shelters; and that the Army Commander won't object to tunnelling personnel being employed in this manner. Last winter No. 256 Tunnelling Co. was employed by the II Corps on the construction of concrete pill boxes with very great success. These shelters are now being used by the Belgian army and have withstood very well the enemy's artillery fire.
>
> 5. I am of the opinion that it is not advisable at any rate for the present to undertake the construction of deep dug-outs in the East Poperinghe system, partly owing to the fact that sufficient labour is not available to find the necessary men to act as tunnellers' mates, and partly because I prefer the concrete shelters, of which I suggest a certain number should be constructed

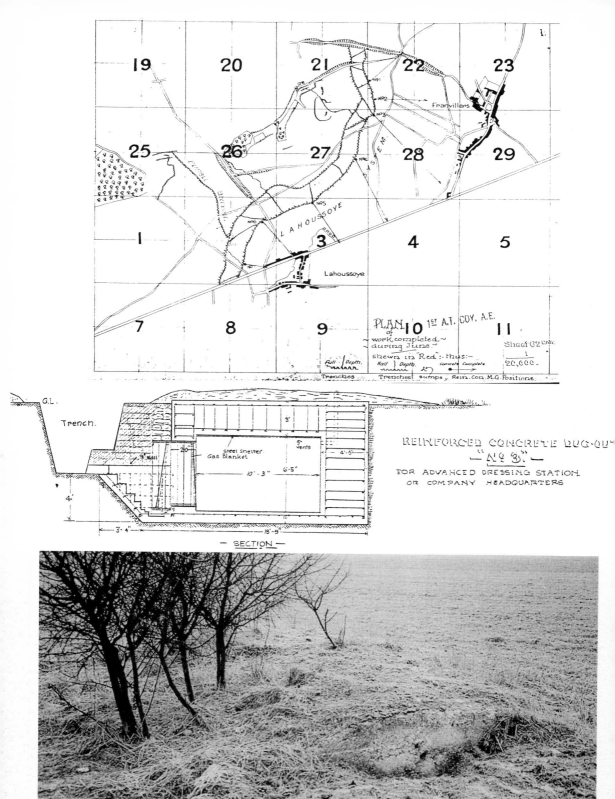

1.

19   20   21   22   23

25   26   27   28   29

Franvillers

LAHOUSSOYE

1   3   4   5

Lahoussoye

7   8   9   10   11

PLAN 10 1ST A.T. COY, A.E.
of
work completed
during June
shewn in "Red": thus:-

Sheet 62 ENE.
1
20,000.

Full Depth.   Half Depth.   Concrete Complete
Trenches   Trenches   Sumps, Rein. Con. M.G. Positions.

G.L.

Trench.

3'

5'
Vents

4'-6"

Steel Shelter
Gas Blanket

9" Wall

10'-3"   6'-5"

REINFORCED CONCRETE DUG-OUT
"No 3"

FOR ADVANCED DRESSING STATION
OR COMPANY HEADQUARTERS

4'

3'-4"   18'-9"

— SECTION —

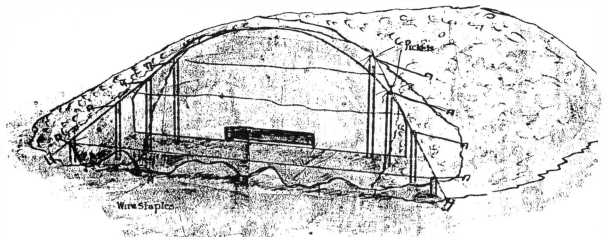

SKETCH OF FRONT CAMOUFLAGE
for M.G. Dugout.

After the 1918 German offensive the British, now on the defensive, officially adopted the use of concrete pill boxes and bunkers. They were constructed in the front, support and rear lines, with defended localities and trench line systems in the back areas − corps, army and GHQ lines. The 1st Australian Division had the task of holding the line in front of and to the north of Villers Bretonneux, which included the road from Amiens to Albert, then in German hands.

To prevent a rapid German advance along the road the Lahoussoye system included a number of pill boxes, sited to cover the road (top left), and shell-proof dug-outs. The design used the steel elephant cupola shelter with a layer of reinforced concrete (centre left), which still survives and can be inspected today (lower left). The 'reinforced MG dugout' design (top), with the embrasure at ground level, allowed for camouflage (below).

before any deep dug-outs are commenced.

The reply from the Second Army major-general gave permission but not encouragement:

There is no objection to the construction of concrete pill boxes instead of tunnelled dug-outs if preferred. Tunnelling personnel is, however, not necessary to construct concrete pill boxes. This work can be undertaken by other troops.

In anticipation of further advances, defence lines were prepared in localities outside the devastated battleground areas. It was felt advantageous, because of camouflage and effectiveness; to construct concrete pill boxes and bunkers in inhabited houses. It was left to the corps commanders to decide on which houses were to be used (or destroyed) and those to be cleared to improve the field of fire. Instructions were issued to the commanders to liaise with the claims commission and the French and Belgian Missions, 'in order to come to some arrangement with the inhabitants or have them evacuated.'

Permission was given for machine-gun emplacements or observation posts to be built in any houses or buildings considered suitable, preferably by arrangement with the inhabitants:

It was suggested that if the houses were occupied the necessity should be explained to the occupiers, who should be interfered with as little as possible.

If this proved impossible, they were instructed to notify the corps liaison officer and claims commission.

In front of the railhead at Poperinghe, 207 Field Company taped out and started constructing the East Poperinghe line for the 34th Division, largely using Moir pill boxes built into existing buildings. These were sited singly and in pairs in two rows at about 250-yard intervals. West of the town the West Poperinghe line, and beyond it the L'Abeele and Watou lines, had many pill boxes and strongpoints made ready for action. Engineers companies of other divisions in this sector were loaned to the infantry to assist in the defence line construction, as were American engineers to gain experience in this kind of work.

256 Royal Engineers Company (Second Army) was busy in front of the railhead town of Hazebrouck, with engineers of the 1st and 2nd American Battalions attached and under instruction

in the art of concrete construction. Further back still the West Hazebrouck line was under development, using many Moir and Second Army pattern pre-cast block bunkers. Work on this line continued until the end of August, 1918.

First Army were well dug-in in the Forest of Nieppe, and the Aire factory was shipping pre-cast pill boxes there via the Lys, Nieppe and Aire canals. Cover from trees eased some of the problems of construction, and a number of standard First Army pattern pill boxes were built on the front edge of the wood by 250 Engineers Company, originally a tunnelling company. Whilst being well built, their standards of construction varied. The remains of one by the Merville-Hazebrouck road shows poor quality with incomplete mixing and inadequate compaction of the concrete, plus leaf prints which are evidence of contamination with weakening materials.

Many standard design pre-cast block pill boxes were built further down the line: St Venant, for example, was well defended by the fourteen built by 250 Royal Engineers Company, 66th Division.

430, 431 and 432 Companies, working on block and *in situ* works on the Hinges-Mont Bernanchon Hill line, reported that they were bored with concrete and wanted another type of work. They had spent all the previous winter converting German pill boxes in the Ypres Salient, 'only to see the works abandoned', and then had Maori New Zealanders working with them as pioneers.

Third Army had fallen back across the 1916 Somme

One of the Mont Bernanchon pill boxes constructed in 1918 by the 66th Division.

Third Army pattern British pill box sited at O'Brien Post in June, 1918. This was the site of the British front line on 1 July, 1916, when the 56th (London) Division carried out a diversionary attack on the Germans in Gommecourt Park opposite. The 1918 defence line stretched to Sailly-au-Bois, where an identical pill box can be found.

battleground, and their new positions between Albert and Arras were stronger than ever. 546 Field Company built 18 pill boxes between Monchy-au-Bois and Gaudimpré in the summer of 1918, but they did not have the luxury of a pre-casting concrete factory like Second and First Armies, so much greater use was made of *in situ* concrete and Moir blocks sent from England. A basic design for a machine-gun pill box consisted of a small underground room and upper chamber for the gun crew, with two embrasures with a central support giving a wide field of fire, the completed construction being camouflaged with sandbags and earth. A good example constructed by the 42nd Division is still on the old 1916 British front line facing the Kaiser's Oak in Gommecourt Park — one of many, it is known as O'Brien Post and was built in June, 1918.

Excellent use was often made of existing buildings and features — a good example stands just outside Colincamps in a barn converted to a pill box with an observation post above. On eighteen successive nights in July, 1918, 428 Field Company

The barn and farmhouse at Colincamps were used by the Royal Engineers attached to the 42nd Division to conceal a concrete machine-gun emplacement and observation post.

ferried, mixed and placed ten tons of material. Built with three-foot-thick foundations and five-foot-thick walls, and with the original building acting as a burster layer, its inhabitants in 1918 would have felt relatively safe and secure.

The German advance had been halted at Albert; while content to let them hold that town, the British did not intend letting them advance further. The village of Hénencourt, just to the west of Albert, was therefore strongly fortified. The 47th Division, holding this part of the line, allocated 517 and 520 Field Companies to the construction of a number of concrete pill boxes in and around Hénencourt between 18 July and 9 August, 1918.

Where the front stabilized towards Villers Bretonneux the

The barn today, showing some minor damage and with a new roof.

Australians, in their usual efficient manner, had planned, built and recorded defences utilizing concrete pill boxes and bunkers. The Albert-Amiens road was covered by a chain of strongly constructed and well camouflaged concrete machine-gun emplacements, built by the 1st Australian Army Troop Company. The design was simple but effective. Fully gas-proofed and partly submerged, it featured a four-feet thick covering of reinforced concrete over a steel lining and a four feet by nine inches loop-hole. A variation, without a loop-hole and with a lower roof level, was used for aid posts and headquarters.

On 8 August, 1918, the Allies moved eastwards from Villers Bretonneux. At this time, the construction as well as the design of pill boxes and bunkers was proceeding at an unprecedented rate. Factories were working to full capacity, with new designs and methods of construction being worked upon. Comparative trials of the Arques and Aire-sur-la-Lys patterns were under way in England, and materials were in plentiful supply.

State-of-the-art defences were detailed, compiled and published as *GHQ Defence Line Specification* in 1918, which highlighted a system intended to be the ultimate in defence design for the all-important general headquarters. This document gave full details of trenches, sections, gaps, configurations and breastworks, plus obstacles such as wire, ditches, road gaps and lines of fire. Standard designs for two types of pill box were included. Type A was for good soil and Type B for swampy soil, with the differences lying mainly in the foundation design. Both were hexagonal and flat-roofed, with two gun-slits and a rear blast wall. This design was used again in Britain in 1940.

The GHQ Line, under construction during the summer of 1918, marked the high point of British defence policy. It showed a major change of thought over the usefulness of concrete bunkers and pill boxes. Taking in many of the ideas from the Hindenburg Line, with some lessons learnt from the German offensive of 21 March, the British hoped it would be impregnable. Some sectors were given local geographical names − the St Omer Line, the Bertangles Line, and so on − although most sectors were known by official names, such as 'B.B. Line'. The total line stretched from the bridgehead at Watten to Amiens, and was intended to ensure that if the Germans pressed forward and captured Ypres,

One of the pill boxes inside, with the observation post above.

Hazebrouck, Arras and Amiens, the ports of Calais and Boulogne would be protected, allowing embarkation of the British rearguard. It gave a defensive zone of about twenty kilometres: the front line and battle zone, reserve line, Army Line and GHQ Line.

With many switches and spurs, the siting of the line took advantage of geological features. An enormous amount of work was done on it throughout the summer of 1918: cast *in situ* and concrete block shelters were constructed at a rapid rate, together with trenches and wiring. Much of the work was still in progress when the next British offensive started, beginning with the Fourth Army in front of Amiens on 8 August. Work continued on the northerly sections of the line until October. At this time the work was largely unfinished, with many trench lines dug only one spade deep as markers, and concrete works incomplete.

Unlike the Germans, the British did not use civilian contractors for construction of this main defence line, even though British contractors were carrying out building and construction work for the army. McAlpine and Sons had crossed the Channel in September, 1914, to build camps for troops around Boulogne and Calais, followed by stables for horses in St Leonard. In April, 1915, they began to build base depôt camps at Etaples, constructing thirty-two camps for training bases, hospitals and reinforcement camps. Many other military contracts followed: hospitals at Camiers and Echengen, salvage depts and Royal Flying Corps camps around St Omer, and map-printing works at Wardreques and Auberque, among others. Tenders for contracts were submitted to the Directorate of Works at the Royal Engineers. While the GHQ Line was being constructed, McAlpine were building ammunition depts, thus freeing Royal Engineers and other military personnel for work on the defence lines.[22]

Concrete dug-outs allowed for three secret emergency exits to the rear trench lines, with 1,000 yards of one-and-a-half-inch-diameter piping connecting to the rear area for pumping in gas in case of enemy occupation. The GHQ Line was a system of continuous and connected defences of varying depths, depending upon the strategic importance of each area, and had many switch-lines, defended localities and strongpoints. As it passed through different army areas variations to standard designs were permitted, but the overall specification was one of solidity and resistance. In its planning and siting, all the lessons learned from detailed studies of the Hindenburg Line were exploited. Its siting anticipated that hitherto all-important towns and villages would be ceded to the Germans.

When the lines at Ypres and Poperinghe had fallen, the armies would fall back to the line between West Hazebrouck and Winnezeele. When this fell, they would continue backwards to a line running from Watten in a south-easterly direction to Thiennes, just behind the Forest of Nieppe. North of this the plan called for flooding the land between Watten and Dunkirk, then on towards Furnes just inside Belgium. The inundation would be controlled from the sluices at Dunkirk, where equipment was installed capable of pumping 345,000 cubic metres of water per day. In some areas canal banks were heightened to aid the water flow, and a pile-dam (and then a second in case the first suffered bomb damage) was built across the Aa Canal at Watten. From here the trenches and pill-box defence lines began. Preliminary flooding was tested on 14 April, 1918; at the request of Maréchal Foch, the French commander-in-chief, fresh water was used in place of sea water, and only to a certain depth.

After Thiennes the line snaked down to Bray-en-Artois; then, to allow for when the Vimy Ridge fell, it took in the villages of Camblain L'Abbé, Frévin Capelle, Agnières, Habarcq, Avesnes-le-Comte and Hauteville, about fifteen kilometres west of Arras. Sweeping south-westwards, across the rear areas of 1916 at Fosseux, Barly, and Saulty to Villers Bocage, the line met the River Somme between Montires and Ailly-sur-Somme. The GHQ Line was built to the west of all those towns the front-line soldier had known to be safe and secure: Ypres (not so safe and secure), Hazebrouck, Béthune, Arras, and even Amiens. But its name was a misnomer: when the time came for this line to defend against an attack, as was surely thought possible and even probable at the time, it would be more than likely that GHQ itself would not be in France or Belgium at all, but away back behind the lines in England.

Moir pill boxes were designed into the GHQ Line system, as was the 'ferro-concrete pancake shelter', a simple form of reinforced concrete shelter. This was built by digging a two-feet-six-inch-wide trench in the form of a square to a depth of six feet and infilling with reinforced concrete, leaving a gap for a doorway. This concrete 'box', with its content of earth, was covered with a two-feet-nine-inch reinforced concrete 'lid'. The earth contents would be excavated through the doorway gap. Allowing for the initial removal of grass and topsoil, the height of the shelters was approximately two feet above ground level. They were designed as 'underground shelters for twelve men, just 5.9″ proof.' The shell-proofing was planned on the basis that:

> It is not as a rule worthwhile attempting to make protection more than 6″ proof, since the physiological effects of concussion resulting from shells of 8″ and upwards is greater than the disruptive.[23]

By the middle of September, 1918, the situation was rapidly changing, and concrete constructions were deemed incompatible with the new 'war of movement'. The recently completed

Engoudsent factory did not start production, and manufacture at Richborough slowed, continuing only to meet one order of 25 Moir pill boxes for shipment to Salonika. On 23 October, 1918, all production ceased. It was now time for the Germans to direct their thoughts to defence.

Standard GHQ Line specification pill box for two machine-guns, constructed as part of the West Hazebrouck defences. The design included piping to pump gas in if the pill box was taken.

20 Hindenburg Line (including the Queant-Drocourt Line), A.P.S.S.8/17 S1383, a report on the layout, construction and wiring of defensive positions.

21 *The Fifth Army* by General Sir Hubert Gough (Chivers, London, reprinted 1968).

22 In addition to much construction work in France, McAlpine also carried out many contracts in Britain for the Ministry of Munitions. Contracts included military camps for troops, ammunition factories, Royal Flying Corps aerodromes and workshops, and completion of a school of aerial gunnery at Loch Doon, where the Royal Engineers had run into problems draining a peat bog. On 7 April, 1918, Roberta McAlpine, daughter of the owner Sir Robert McAlpine, married Major Richard Lloyd George of the Royal Engineers, eldest son of the British Prime Minister.

23 GHQ Specification No. 4 published in June, 1918, embodying and revising Specifications Nos. 1 to 3. For distribution to corps headquarters, it gave detailed advice on the siting and construction of the GHQ Line − Britain's last line of defence before the Channel ports.

CHAPTER SEVEN

Coastal Defences

At the beginning of the First World War most of Britain's coastal defences were concentrated in the south and south-east, the main threat for such a long time having come from France, with Imperial Germany considered as a potential invader only in 1910. It was thought wise to prepare some defence for the coast further north, as protection from both a possible landing and the threat of naval bombardment. Royal Navy vessels patrolled the east and north-east coasts, and in the summer of 1914 the Grand Fleet moved its base to Scapa Flow.

Defences on the coastline were increased and modernized as the war progressed, concentrating on heavy gun emplacements, trenches and infantry positions, the latter particularly in East Anglia and Kent. Infantry positions constructed later in 1917 and 1918 contained small machine-gun emplacements or pill boxes, as these had been found helpful in providing strong defensive positions.

All major east coast estuaries were considered potential landing spots and were defended as such. The Thames estuary was heavily fortified from earlier times, but the Wash and the Humber estuary were unprotected and defences were provided accordingly. The Tyne estuary, a major port area importing and exporting vast amounts of materials, especially coal, was also a centre for shipbuilding and repair, and of considerable strategic importance. Originally defended by Royal Navy ships based at Rosyth in Scotland, in 1917 heavy guns in fixed batteries of reinforced concrete were constructed, with each battery able to defend itself from attack. Further batteries were built north and south of the estuary to complete the defences.

At Hartley, north of the estuary, five miles from Tynemouth, Roberts Battery enjoyed a comprehensive field of fire, except for an area just behind the Saint Mary's Lighthouse. It consisted of concrete gun-bases, underground ammunition stores, and heavy

The pill box guarding the coastal approach to Roberts Battery at Hartley. It was sited to prevent an infantry or marine attack on the 12-inch heavy guns. The pill box gun-slits incorporated protective metal plates.

12-inch guns which had originally been mounted on HMS Illustrious. Concrete perimeter walls with built-in defensive positions featuring loop-holes to direct small-arms fire enclosed the battery; the loop-holes were fitted with metal protective plates especially designed for rifles. The battery and enveloping pill box was considered to be a self-contained defensive position.

South of the estuary Kitchener Battery was of similar construction, also fitted with 12-inch guns from HMS Illustrious. Notably, due to manpower shortages, the battery was constructed by local female labour. Both batteries were controlled and commanded from a six-storey building to the rear of the Grand Hotel in Tynemouth itself, giving an unobstructed view of the Tyne approaches. Little evidence of either battery is left today, but the pill box at Roberts Battery is still in existence. It shows a sound design geared to its purpose: a structure with relatively thin walls, providing cover from rifle or machine-gun fire.

Further south the enemy submarine threat was on the increase, with mounting shipping losses in the English Channel. Maritime traffic between English and French ports, especially those at Boulogne, Calais and Dunkirk, was extremely hazardous. The Dover Patrol was forever busy trying to keep the problem under control, and a major part of its working day was spent laying surface and below-surface minefields. There were minefields off the Belgian coast, as well as lines of nets and mines strung between Deal and Dunkirk, and between Folkestone and Cap Gris Nez. All these were effective, but not enough.

The Admiralty, under the strong influence of its civil engineer-in-chief, Alex Gibb, was fully convinced that reinforced concrete was the best material for constructing coastal defences. The Admiralty's faith in concrete led to new thinking on the submarine threat, and a plan was devised to improve control over the strings of nets and mines in the Channel. A chain of 14 concrete forts would be floated out and sunk into position in a line across the Channel. A prototype fort was tested off

Anti-submarine defence forts under construction in Shoreham Harbour in 1918. After hostilities ceased, one was floated out and positioned; it was called Nab Tower, and became a navigational and weather station.

Portsmouth, with disastrous results - it turned over and sank.

Rapid design changes were instigated which, combined with the use of the latest developments in electrical apparatus, led to a new style of fort. An amendment to the plan meant that only eight of them would be required. Construction began in Shoreham harbour, using reinforced concrete in a hexagonal design with a 60-metre wide base and a height of 61 metres. The forts would sit in 55 metres of water, and each weighed approximately 10,000 tonnes. (A similar principle of casting, floating and sinking was used sixty years later in North Sea oil platform construction.) Two of the eight forts were completed by the time hostilities ceased in November, 1918. On 12 September, 1920, one of them was towed into the Solent and sunk as a lighthouse, now known as Nab Tower.

On the coast in occupied Belgium the Germans had built numerous heavy gun batteries to defend against an Allied landing and maintain the freedom of the sea for their submarines and other vessels using the strategically important ports at Ostend and Zeebrugge. The German *Marinekorps* built thirty-six reinforced concrete batteries, incorporating ammunition storage, shell-proof bunkers for the crews, observation posts made of bomb-proof concrete, and iron shielding for the guns. Well camouflaged and affording each other covering fire, the batteries generally featured four guns ranging between 4-inch and 15-inch calibre, with smaller anti-aircraft guns of 3-inch calibre.

These batteries eventually fell from the rear, when the garrison destroyed the guns and retreated on 15 and 16 October, 1918, with all hope of holding the coast lost. The Belgian Army occupied them for the last weeks of the war. After the Armistice the batteries were stripped for scrap, although some of their remnants were strengthened and refortified as part of the Atlantic Wall in the 1940s. The only one remaining is Aachen Battery at Raversijde, which has survived destruction because it sits on land owned by Prince Karel of the Belgian Royal Family.

GAZETTEER

In the region of 300 concrete bunkers, pill boxes, observation posts and gun emplacements exist on what was at times the British sector of the Western Front. This guide extends from the Belgian coast in the north to St Quentin in France in the south.

These memorials to the static nature of the First World War are not necessarily permanent, and the ones surviving today do so by luck, as few exist in preserved areas or museums. Since the 1920s they have been disappearing, many to make way for roads and buildings, others to release the land on which they sit, yet others because they were eyesores or were in the way of farmers. In Belgium the army sometimes killed two birds with one stone, by blowing up concrete bunkers filled with left-over explosives from the war which had been ploughed up in the fields. Henry Williamson listened to pill boxes being blown up around Brandhoek in 1927.[24] When land was being put back to use after the war, concrete monoliths were a good source of road stone, especially valuable in areas such as Flanders. Nevertheless, some were retained for the tourist trade, and some because they were likely to be of use to farmers. But most survived simply because the cost of destroying them was just too much.

In 1933 the British Legion published a guide to the pill boxes of Flanders.[25] At the time it was incomplete and since then more than half of those noted between the Pilkem Ridge and the village of Messines have disappeared. Most of the constructions shown in the general tourist guides published in the years after the First World War, Michelin Guides, *Twenty Years After*,[26] *I Was There*,[27] and so on, have also gone. The most recent guide book showing locations of bunkers in the Ypres Salient in the 1960s is *Ieper en de frontstreek*, but again many mentioned in this publication have been demolished since.[28] Each year the numbers decrease.

This guide gives some information on those which remain, although it cannot be taken as complete as many were built well behind the front line, in woods, barns, hillsides, and other secluded spots. Visitors to pill boxes, bunkers, observation posts or shelters are reminded that many are on private land and this should be respected. Most farmers and landowners will happily allow inspection if asked. It is worth bearing in mind that danger lurks around some bunkers through extruding steel bars, difficult exits, slippery footholds and the ever-present possibility of live shells and small-arms ammunition.

It is possible to determine which side constructed or adopted a pill box, shelter or observation post. Loop-holes and observation slits will generally face the enemy, as will the rear wall of bunkers. The door is probably the most significant indication, nearly always pointing back to the constructors' own rear areas: German constructions generally have a doorway facing eastwards, or between north-north-east and south-south-east, whereas British doorways face west.

There is often a difference in the colour of the concrete: that of most German constructions is usually darker than that of British pill boxes. The latter were generally made with light-coloured Portland cement supplied mainly from the Medway cement works, whereas the Germans used cement from their own cement works such as that in Heidelberg, or from works in occupied territory like Obourg and Antwerp. Continental practice was to grind blast-furnace slag with the cement clinker, producing a darker cement. Some British cement was used by the Germans, supplied by the Dutch who had purchased it from the British for resale, as described in Chapter Two.

From North to South

The most northerly concrete constructions were on the Belgian coast: large gun batteries and a number of bunkers and observation posts. Of the thirty-six batteries built there the only one remaining is the Aachen Battery, overlooking the beach at Raversijde, but it is much altered after being adapted into part of Hitler's Atlantic Wall in the Second World War. The original works can still be seen, surviving only because the land on which it sits is privately owned. The site has recently been converted into an open-air museum.

On the N34, the Belgian coast road, the outskirts of Westende-Bad embrace Rosiers Bunker, complete with a 1915 name-plate. Many bunkers in this area are from the Second World War, as are the large ones at Groote Bamburgh Farm outside Lombartzijde, although a First World War German bomb-proof shelter is sited between these points, used as a shelter by civilians in the 1940s and today for dry storage.

Knokke-Heist on the Belgian coast was the starting point of a long line of defences, built along the Dutch border in anticipation of the perceived British landings in neutral Holland. Large numbers were constructed in 1916 by the German Marinekorps *and lightly manned. Many were built into dykes and still exist (see photo on page 94). This observation post can be found in the border fort behind Knokke-Heist, reached by taking a small road off the N376 at Schapenbrug, and continuing further along the border.*

There are many bunkers along sections of the Belgian border with The Netherlands, especially between Knokke-Heist and Maldegem. It is often difficult to gain access to these and directions may be required, as several can only be reached by tracks and by-roads leading off the N49. Nearby, south of the N318, is Ruby Farm, a German command bunker with much wood lining still on the ceiling.

On the N234 towards Lovie, Block House Farm retains its field battery command post.

The fort of Nieuwendamme, a strongpoint with good all-round views, still has its block built bunkers watching over the old British lines.

Other bunkers, such as Rank Post on the edge of Nieuland Polder, are difficult to visit because of the many small waterways thereabouts.

India Rubber House in Nieuport gave shelter on the Redan and is now a storage for sea-dredged sand and gravel.

West of Nieuport on the N396 is Triangle Wood, with many bunkers in the adjoining field. Probably French, all are to a standard design.

On the N367 from Nieuport to St Joris, a small British bunker can be seen on the right.

Along the N39 approaching Wulpen is a high observation post. The Stonebakkery chimney still commands excellent visibility over the surrounding land (see page 59).

Between Nieuport and Ypres there are several bunkers from the time when this was a Belgian sector. An observation tower in the centre of Pervijze, originally the house of a church official, has its tower strengthened by concrete blocks. The brickwork addition at the top probably dates from the 1940s' occupation.

At Stuivekenskerke the church confirms that such buildings were not immune from being turned into a pill box if in the right location. Nearby is the Boyau de la Mort, concreted after the war to commemorate the types of trenches and revetments of the time. Klerken, in the same area on the German side of the front, has a four-storey observation tower built into a house in the middle of the village, an example of a well-camouflaged observation post. The result of a hit just by the observation slit shows the strength of the construction.

The ruined windmill on the road to Houthulst shows a good observation site.

This bunker in the grounds of Boesinghe Château, the largest remaining example of British concrete construction in Belgium, was the battle headquarters for several battalions of the Guards Division. The Guards took over the area in June, 1917, and the attached Royal Engineers (75 and 76 Field Companies) constructed shell-proof command posts for the coming battle. Prior to the start of the main attack, a number of operations and trench raids were planned in this bunker. On the night of 28-29 July, 1917, a raiding party of the 1st Battalion Irish Guards seized a German blockhouse (Bois Farm), capturing a machine-gun and killing or taking prisoner the garrison. Other battalions of the Guards used the bunker shortly after, and the Grenadiers planned subsequent attacks here. The bunker was used by various units over the next 15 months, and was handed over to the Belgians for the final offensive in September, 1918. Hessian sandbag formwork is still evident, as is some of the brickwork of the original Château. It has two chambers, which still show traces of whitewash on the inside. Also in Boesinghe on the main street is a British observation post, now covered in ivy, with a German trench mortar on top of the roof. Built for artillery observation, it gave a view over the canal and bridge to the German lines on the rising ground of Pilkem Ridge.

Travelling south, the British sector starts at Boesinghe just past Dixmuide. On the main road through the village, overlooking the bridge to Pilkem, is a British observation post built inside a house with a German mortar, a *Kleine Bertha*, sitting on top. A few hundred yards away, in the woods of Boesinghe Château, just up the lane behind the church, is a large, double-chambered, British bunker showing camouflage, and with remains of whitewash on the inside. It is the largest remaining British bunker in the Ypres Salient.

The British hospital in the canal bank at Essex Farm on the N369 north of Ypres is worth visiting. The attention to detail in the concrete shows the quality of workmanship, and the fleurs-de-lis decorating the inside walls of the end bunker indicates an attempt at providing home comforts, although it is highly likely that it would not have survived a direct hit from a heavy shell. Remains of bunkers further along the embankment illustrate its wide use as service and living quarters for troops.

The Pilkem Ridge, eastwards from Boesinghe over the canal bridge towards Langemarck, has many defensive positions constructed by the Germans between 1915 and 1917, and by the British from September 1917 to summer 1918.

On the left over the railway line towards Langemarck in what was Wood 16 stands a large light-signalling station, known as the Viking Ship on account of its shape. Taken firstly by the French and then occupied by the Guards Division, it was built by men of the German *Marinekorps* commanded by an officer called Ziegler, using reinforcing steel taken from engineering works in Belgium. The rear doors were blasted in by the British and the damage exposes all kinds and shapes of steel profiles. The large window, for transmitting signals, shows the importance of light for communications. (see photograph on page 80)

At the next crossroads (Charpentier Crossroads), turn right and there is a small bunker on the left. Right again at the next junction and a few yards to the right is a German battery position which shows how a rear door could be concreted up for protection after it was taken (probably by the British 256 Tunnelling Company). It is an example of the Germans' use of round steel bars wired together for strengthening. Further on the left, in what was

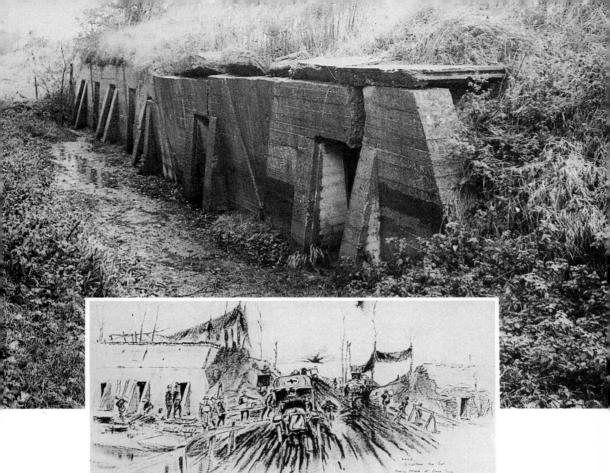

Essex Farm dressing station in the canal bank north of Ypres saw much activity during the war. Protected by the embankment, it was a natural position for administrative and operational centres. Several divisions held this sector in 1916, when it was a relatively quiet area, and each improving the dressing station. It was made shrapnel-proof in May, 1915, and later shell-proof by Royal Engineers of 458 West Riding Company of the 49th Division, whose memorial is nearby. It was taken over and manned by the 1/2nd and 1/3rd Highland Field Ambulances, Royal Army Medical Corps, on 16 June, 1917, in preparation for the Messines offensive. It treated many men during the third battle of Ypres, and was the target of much shelling due to its location at Bridge No. 4 over the canal. On 10 July, 1917, heavy shelling buried eight stretcher-bearers and damaged a motor ambulance. On 7 August, 1917, the hospital was handed over to the 11th Division. Essex Farm is known as the site where Lieutenant-Colonel John McCrae wrote In Flanders Fields *while stationed there with the Royal Canadian Medical Corps. A feature of the bunkers is the fleurs-de-lis decorations on the walls of the end compartment. A contemporary sketch shows the dressing station and bridge in July, 1917.*

125

Major's Farm, are two bunkers, the larger one an example of how the British turned around a German bunker. Over the brow of the hill to the east, a half-sunken bunker at Colonel's Farm bears the mark of its builders over the doorway inside.

Around Langemarck, west of the Pilkem Ridge, the German military cemetery contains some solid, durable bunkers and tank stops.

Over the Broenbeek to the north, sited for maximum advantage (the stream was not easily crossed in 1917), is a pill box with impressions of camouflage in the concrete. In front is the memorial to the 34th Division Royal Artillery and Royal Engineers, who used it as a base. A hundred yards further on are the remains of a concrete pill box, standing about three feet high, with another one a hundred yards behind, up the small road to the side. This group was an obstacle to the Guards Division, preventing them from crossing the stream during several attacks in August, 1917. The 29th Division, who relieved the Guards, tried to ford the stream and take the pill boxes on 16 August, but failed. The Germans remained in their strongpoints, watching the British over the widening water. The Guards tried again on 27 August, but repeated heavy shelling had made the stream, carrying extra water after a period of continuous rain, a wide swamp, with no clear definition between land and water. On 9 September they managed to cross the liquid mud, subdue the enemy and capture the pill boxes. Further advance was not possible and the positions were held as forward posts by the Irish Guards. On 13 September the German 65th Reserve Infantry Regiment counterattacked, forcing the Guards to retire to the southern edge of the stream.

Back to the main road and, after turning left through Koekuit, the road bends sharply to the left. Just before the bend, on the right, is Vee Bend bunker.

In the summer of 1918 the British, on the defensive and accepting that reinforced concrete shelters were a good means of protection, planned and built many in front of and around Ypres as well, as between the town and Poperinghe. Most of these have now gone, but two Moir pill boxes are left intact on the ramparts overlooking the Dickebusch road.

Vee Bend bunker is in a farmyard just past Koekuit, north of Langemarck, and named by the British after its location by a sharp bend in the road. Lieutenant Ernst Junger of the 73rd Hanoverian Fusilier Regiment described passing through Koekuit and sheltering from British shell fire in fortified houses when he was on his way to Langemarck to fight the British near the Broembeek.[29] On 9 October, 1917, this blockhouse held up and repelled an attack by the 1st Guards Brigade. Later that day the Coldstream Guards advanced and surrounded the building, capturing thirty-five men and three machine-guns. The bunker was then used as a forward observation post by the British. P. J. Cambell used the bunker for artillery observation, describing it as 'a good pill box'.[30] The bunker was later used as a shelter by the Highland Light Infantry.

A number of standard British concrete shell-proof shelters, curved concrete arches cast over corrugated elephant-iron inner shells, are in the fields and woods west and south of Ypres, in the area between Elverdinghe and Dickebusch. Two are at what was Anzac Camp a few hundred yards from the Kruisstraathoek crossroads. Another, with sandbag imprints of the outer layer, is at what was Zillebeke Lake Siding by the sharp bend in the Ypres-Verbrandenmolen road. Machine Gun Farm Depôt was a railway siding on the ground where the D38 main road now runs, between Ypres and Vlamertinghe. The Machine Gun Farm building, also known as Bibge Cottage, was used as a casualty clearing station for most of the war. In May, 1918, the 57th Field Company Royal Engineers converted it into shell-proof headquarters for a brigade of the 49th Division. The concrete bunker itself is still inside the barn.

After the fighting in 1917, and the spring offensive further south in 1918, the British withdrew to within one mile of Ypres. Strong defences were built with many pill boxes, some of them using the Sir Ernest Moir pattern (see page 52). Two remain on the Ypres ramparts overlooking the Dickebusch road. Constructed by 208 Field Company Royal Engineers for machine gunners of the 34th Division in August 1918, the steel revolving protective rings and Vickers machine-gun brackets have been removed, and a brick wall and houses today block the field of fire to the German lines.

Near the village of Wieltje, north-east of Ypres, are a number of German pill boxes dating from 1916 and 1917. By Cambrai crossroads, the first crossroads after the motorway, three pill boxes are sited in the field on the right. Along what was Cambrai Trench, these, together with another two on the other side of the motorway, are the remaining examples of several dozen which were constructed in 1916 and 1917 within 100 or 200 yards of the British front line. This Cambrai area was the front line in the summer of 1918 after the British withdrew, the only section of the 1915-1917 line which was also that of 1918 line. Turn left at the crossroads, and in a field on the left, 200 yards on, is another 1916 pill box, Pickelhaube House. It stands 50 yards behind the

German front line and was captured by the 55th Division on 31 July, 1917. Pickelhaube House remained in British hands and was part of the front line during the summer of 1918.

Several hundred pill boxes and bunkers were built in this area by the Germans from the summer of 1915 onwards. Few remain, but, whilst some of those that do are only just recognizable in woods and fields, some are fine examples of solid protection, making good use of what features there were at the time. Gourmier Farm, a bunker built into a farmhouse, was captured by the 6th Black Watch on 31 July, 1917. The Germans inflicted heavy casualties on the attackers, who took twenty prisoners, two machine-guns and a field gun.

Take the small road between Ypres and Pilkem, turn right at the last crossroads, named 5 Chemins after an estaminet that stood there, and follow the road for three miles. It carries a plaque to men of the 38th Welsh Division who were killed in various actions in this vicinity. Between Gourmier Farm and 5 Chemins crossroads is Hindenburg Farm, with a bunker alongside the modern barn. Just over the road are the remains of a small construction demolished by shell fire.

Machine Gun Farm (Bibge Cottage), by the N38 Ypres by-pass near Brielen, is typical of many bunkers built into farms and houses. The steel beams protruding from the walls of the barn reinforce a thick concrete inner roof. Most of Machine Gun Farm was taken up by light rail sidings and stores areas. The farmhouse was a dressing station before rear defences were reorganized with the anticipated spring offensive in 1918. It was then designated as brigade headquarters for units of the 41st Division, which held the Brielen Defence Line. It now houses cattle.

Polygon Wood, reached by taking a side road southwards out of Zonnebeke, contains a total of six concrete bunkers. Directly in the centre of the wood, halfway down the main ride facing the Australian Memorial at the Buttes cemetery, and a hundred yards to the north of the path, is a large, double-chambered pill box showing signs of direct hits. This was taken by the 56th Battalion, 5th Australian Division, attacking at 5.50am on 26 September, 1917, just as the sun rose. The German occupiers at first resisted strongly, but the Australians who surrounded and captured the pill box reported that on surrendering they came out as 'whimpering boys, holding out arms full of souvenirs'. The pill box was named Scott Post, in memory of Lieutenant-Colonel Humphrey Scott, commander of the 56th Battalion, who was killed at the Buttes three days later. The British used it as a battalion headquarters during the battle of Broodseinde. The 8th Leicesters made themselves comfortable here after the battle, and it was incorporated as part of the defence improvement scheme in the spring of 1918. The remains of another bunker taken by the 56th Battalion at the same time lie 150 yards due south of Scott Post.

Some 250 yards north-east of Scott Post, and 150 yards from the cemetery, are two small concrete dug-outs. These were constructed by the 4th Field Company, New Zealand Engineers, as four-man shelters in January, 1918. Just inside the southern edge of the wood, 300 yards east of the car park, are the ruins of two more pill boxes. These held up the 31st Australian Battalion under Lieutenant Wilson and the 59th Australian Battalion under Lieutenant McDonald for some time on 26 September, 1917, before they were eventually taken. Sixty men of the 229th Reserve Infantry Regiment and their commander, Hauptmann Fischer, were taken prisoner. The pill boxes were taken in what later became a classic style, with men moving round to the rear entrance (instead of trying to take it head on) and bombing the doorway whilst a Lewis gun was trained on and fired at the loop-hole.

On the road from Ypres turn left just before entering the village of St Julien, and to the right behind the fence of the field bordering the road is a German command bunker. Described by Edwin Campion Vaughan as having about eight baby elephant cubicles,

Hackney Villa, a large German bunker to the west of St Julien, shows the size and extent of many such constructions in the Ypres Salient. Built as a command centre and used as a field hospital, it has been severely damaged by shell fire. Of the original eight compartments only four remain, linked by the corridor, and two others are ruined. Edwin Campion Vaughan described sitting in one of the compartments on 25 August, 1917, when it was in British hands.[31] A direct hit on the bunker caused a stack of flares in an adjacent compartment to ignite, and all occupants dashed out into the corridor. Vaughan left this bunker to capture Springfield pill box nearby with men of the 1/8th Warwickshire Regiment. Whilst Springfield pill box no longer exists, one of the Boilerhouse group Vaughan sheltered in can still be found in the back garden of a house in the village. This one was captured by the 13th Royal Sussex Regiment, 39th Division, on the opening day of the Passchendaele offensive on 31 July, 1917. The Germans retired over the Steenbeck, fifty yards behind, into the village of St Julien, where resistance stiffened and their 50th Division counterattacked, forcing the Royal Sussex to fall back over the river to the bunker (which they retained as a front line defensive position).

it received a direct hit which ignited a stack of flares in the next cubicle to the one he occupied. Looking north-east, just over the Steenbeck, in the back garden of a house on the Poelcapelle road is one of the group of buildings also mentioned by Edwin Campion Vaughan as containing the Boilerhouse, a squat, round-topped shelter with an inner galvanized-steel lining.

Take the road south out of St Julien to Fortuinhoek, an area well covered by machine-guns housed in the Pond Farm pill box, about 300 yards to the left. A mile past Pond Farm in the direction of Passchendaele, on the left at the junction marked s'Gravenstafel is a British concrete shelter, named Wimbledon, built into the lee of the rising ground. (photograph page 97)

Pond Farm pill box, by the crossroads south of St Julien, was captured by the 55th (West Lancashire) Division on 31 July, 1917, after the Liverpool Scottish and South Lancashire Battalions had been held up by machine-gun fire from it. The Lancastrians consolidated the position and pressed on to Kansas Cross, 1,000 yards further on. The ground taken and the strongpoint at Pond Farm had to be given up after a counterattack by the 60th Reserve Regiment, supported by aircraft bombing and machine-gunning from low level. The British front line remained 300 yards in front of the farm (just about where the crossroads is today) for the next two weeks. On 16 August a platoon of the 14th Irish Rifles, 36th (Ulster) Division, under Lieutenant Ledlie, made a determined attempt to take the pill box but were beaten back. On 22 August D Company of the 14th Battalion attacked and captured the position, lost it to a counterattack, and retook it assisted by C Company at 12 noon that day. Captain Tubbs, Second Lieutenants Davies and Blyths and sixteen other ranks were killed, and fifty-two men wounded in the attack. The pill box inflicted many casualties on the 21st Oxfordshire and Buckinghamshires, who were trying to advance on the right. Their battalion war diary states, 'The Hun fought well when protected with concrete'.

The pill boxes in Tyne Cot cemetery saw some of the hardest fighting and most adverse conditions of the First World War. The two pill boxes in front of the cemetery (named Irksome and The Barnacle after their capture) were sited next to Dab Trench, 50 yards behind the present road, part of the Flandern I Stellung *of Staden-Zonnebeke Line. The area now occupied by the cemetery was the objective (the Blue Line) of the 40th (Tasmanian) Battalion, 3rd Division, Australian Imperial Forces, for an attack on 4 October, 1917 (the battle of Broodseinde). Prior to the attack the weather was fine and dry, but rain caused the ground to become greasy, giving the Australians problems in reaching their jumping-off line. While waiting in the rain for the attack to begin, a heavy German bombardment caused many casualties. At 8.10am on the morning of 4 October the 40th Battalion attacked the pill boxes. Heavy machine-gun fire checked the advance, but the Tasmanians managed to work around the back. Sergeant McGee won a VC by shooting the crew of one machine-gun on top of a pill box, and Captain Dumaresq was awarded the MC for bravery in hand-to-hand fighting. The pill boxes were taken one by one. 'Many pill boxes very little damaged by artillery fire, manned by two to four machine-guns. On being rushed the enemy surrendered without making a fight of it, many dead were to be seen outside these structures.'[32] Fifteen machine-guns and two* Minenwerfers *were captured. Apart from the awards to Sergeant McGee and Captain Dumaresq, another officer, Lieutenant Boyes, won the MC, and one DCM and nine MMs were awarded around the pill boxes. The two front pill boxes became the front of the line, consolidated by A and B Companies, whose machine-gun beat off an attack by the 9th Bavarian Infantry Regiment. The furthest pill box, now under the Cross of Sacrifice, remained in German hands for another five days. Another advance was planned for 9 October, when the 66th Division was to attack and capture the ground behind the pill boxes and press on to the edge of Passchendaele village. Battalions of the Manchesters, East Lancashires and Lancashire Fusiliers had difficulty in reaching the front line. Rain and heavy shelling made the ground impossible to cover. The attack began at 5.20am with a much depleted force (the 2/6th Lancashire Fusiliers were still en route*

three miles away). Despite the problems, patrols of the 2/8th East Lancashires entered Passchendaele, but had to retire under withering machine-gun fire. Men of the 66th Division held the area around Tyne Cot, sheltering in flooded shell-holes and behind pill boxes under continuous artillery and machine-gun fire until relieved at 10pm on 10 October by a reduced force of Australian troops. Two companies of the 2/6th Lancashire Fusiliers stayed in the line until 6am the following morning. They reported that 'there was exceptionally heavy shelling (hostile) from 3.00am to 4.30am.'[33] The 3rd Australian Division launched another assault from the Tyne Cot pill boxes on 12 October. As with the 66th Division, the village was reached by small numbers of troops who then had to fall back to the starting line. Whilst Tyne Cot was in the front line the Germans counterattacked frequently to try to regain the position. On 12 October, when the Australians were massing for their assaults, the 2nd Battalion, 10th Bavarian Reserve Infantry Regiment advanced through the British artillery barrage before being repulsed. At 11.00am the 8th Jäger Regiment, 195 Division, was also beaten back. Other unsuccessful attempts followed. Tyne Cot was held by the Canadian Corps from 18 October, with the pill boxes being used as advanced dressing stations by the 4th Canadian Division. On 30 October the 3rd Bavarian Infantry Regiment (11th Bavarian Division) were repulsed at 4.45pm and then the 464 Infantry Regiment (238 Division) at 6pm. The Canadians launched a successful attack on the high ground of the village on 10 November. The pill boxes remained in active use through the winter, the medical units of the 50th and 33rd Divisions burying their dead in the surrounding mud (thus starting the cemetery). The graves and bunkers were given up in April 1918, when the British withdrew closer to Ypres, to be retaken by the Belgians on 28 September, 1918.

Possibly the most famous pill boxes in the salient are those in Tyne Cot cemetery. Originally part of a larger group, they show the excellent cover and field of fire all the way to Ypres. In the garden of a house by the road junction to the south-east of Tyne Cot are the remains of another pill box, one of the same group as those in the cemetery. This one covered the railway where it crossed the road (known as Dash Crossing). Following the small road along the rear wall for 250 yards and on the right in the garden of a smallholding is a large, semi-prone concrete monolith. This is the remains of Hillside Farm, a large blockhouse captured by the Australians on 12 October, 1917. It is the most easterly pill box remaining in the salient of 1917. Some do remain in what was the German forward area, just beyond the limit of the British advance.

North out of Passchendaele at Vindictive Crossroads (500 yards along the N303), Oostnieukirke is signposted to the right. Three-quarters of a mile along this road, at the second turning

Potsdam, a group of pill boxes built into and straddling the Ypres-Roulers railway, covered the approach to Zonnebeke and the Passchendaele Ridge They were named Potsdam after a farm between the railway and the Ypres-Zonnebeke road. The Germans named the group to the north of the line Lindenhof *after the same farm, and numbered it* Wida V 66. *The group to the south of the railway line they called* Schwabenhof. *Bunkers in the embankment connected the two sides: flanking fire was given to the Brandenberg strongpoint (Bremen Redoubt to the British — now the site of a brickworks), as well as to Zonnebeke Redoubt to the south. On 16 August, 1917, the 7th Irish Rifles, 16th Division, were held back by fire from here. They recorded that shell fire had little or no effect — so strong were the pill boxes that their machine-guns actually maintained fire as the barrage passed over them.[34] The 2nd Middlesex Regiment, 8th Division, took casualties as they tried to pass on the other side of the railway. On 20 September, 1917, the 9th (Scottish) Division was ordered to capture Potsdam. Specific pill boxes were given numbers — R1, R2, R3 and so on — for the attack. In one case the attackers tried to put a grenade through the loop-hole, but the occupiers blocked it by ramming in a pack while still keeping the machine-gun firing. Captain Reynolds of the Royal Scots squeezed a phosphorous bomb past the obstruction into the pill box, which caused the defenders to surrender. He was awarded the VC for his action. Potsdam provided shelter for Allied troops during later stages of the fighting. The 44th Australian Battalion had their headquarters here for the Tyne Cot attack on 4 October; the 66th Division, with the assistance of Maori Pioneers of the New Zealand Division, wired the position as a strongpoint in case of counterattacks. The 2/5th Manchester Regiment had their headquarters here, whilst holding the Tyne Cot pill boxes as front line positions. The bunker remains in the embankment today are the rear wall of the one designated R1 for the Scottish attack.*

on the right (named Nachtegaalestraate), is a small crossroads. Directly in front, hidden by bushes, is a concrete machine-gun post. Turn right and, following the road round to the left, in the garden of a house is a bunker with its doorway bricked up to allow for water storage. Both were within machine-gun distance of the Canadians who took Passchendaele, and probably helped hold up their advance. The garrisons also held the 2nd Lincolns and 2nd Royal Berkshires, 8th Division, who attempted to take the German positions midway between here and Vindictive Crossroads on the night of 1/2 December, 1917.

If the British had been able to push further eastwards they would have come up against many other fortified farms and buildings. Some can still be found. On the outskirts of De Ruiter near Roeselare is a bunker similar to the ones near Passchendaele. Another guards the crossing (Snipe Crossing) where the railway spanned the Roeselare-Moorslede road.

The Roeselare-Menin road (the N32) was strongly defended and studded with pill boxes in a wide belt on either side. The Germans planned this as a major defence line, and some of the constructions remain. Midway along the main road is the hamlet and crossroads of St Pieter, from where a side road winds directly to Ledegem. From this road a small road forks right to some industrial units. On the right, fronting onto a barn, is Lord's Farm pill box, with three chambers and an observation hatch with a steel ladder set into the wall stands. It features an embrasure for small arms to cover the rear entrance. In October, 1918, Lord's Farm slowed the advance of the 9th Scottish Division, who were then held up again at Ledegem.

On the south-west of this village, going towards Dadizeele, is a large German bunker sited adjacent to the old railway lines, with a rear extension and observation post. This was probably an artillery command post, and shows signs of damage by German shells after capture by the British. In Dadizeele cemetery is a standard pattern pill box for the area, with two chambers and steps to a rear fire platform (and now used by gardeners for storage). [see photo page 37] Almost identical models are found on the southern edge of Geluwe, part of the same defence line.

Bois Quarante, reached by taking the road to Vierstraat out of Wyteschaete and turning right after about one mile, was so named because of the 40-metre contour line which runs through the wood. It was named Croonart Wald *by the Germans after a chapel which stood on the edge of the wood — a chapel painted by Adolf Hitler in one of his leisure moments while serving here. The chapel is no longer there, but the wood still embraces several bunkers made of concrete blocks. On 7 June, 1917, Bois Quarante was held by the German 2nd Division. They were ready and waiting to be relieved when the British 19th Division attacked after a heavy bombardment of explosives, gas shells and incendiary oil drums. The bunkers were taken without a struggle, the captors recording that many Germans soon surrendered, and 'very few of them put up a fight'. As the wood was in a fairly quiet zone (three miles behind the front), the bunkers were used as accommodation by the various troops quartered here. The 1st Australian Division used them during the winter of 1917-1918. In April, 1918, the Germans rapidly approached the woods, recapturing the bunkers from the 21st Division on 25 April, 1918, and occupying them for the rest of the summer. The wood was maintained as a museum until recent years. The owner claimed that Adolf Hitler won his Iron Cross in this area, and that he had been based in the bunkers in 1917 and revisited them in 1940. He also claimed that a painting he owned of the old Cronaert Chapel had been painted by Adolf Hitler, the aspect of the painting indicating that it had been painted from alongside one of the bunkers on the edge of the wood. Following the owner's death, the trenches and tunnels have fallen into disrepair, and details of the whereabouts of Hitler's painting seem to have been buried with him.*

Lord's Farm, built behind the farmyard which fronts the N32 Menin-Roulers road, is one of the few surviving of many built to the same design along this defence line. It was captured by Scots of the 9th Division in October, 1918.

The line continued south of Wervicq and the River Lys, with many of the concrete defences intact. South of Wervicq-Sud on the D9 is La Montagne, where the woods on the right have pill boxes on the westward slope of the hill. Also in these woods, close to the apex of the hill, is one of the few surviving stone-built German memorials. Three-quarters of a mile further down the D9 turn right toward Le Long Champs: bunkers and gun emplacements are sited on both sides of the road. After 600 yards turn left and after another 600 yards, between Le Gavre and Les Trois Fetus, on the right are three machine-gun positions. West of the D64 between Linselles and Bousbecque, at Le Belcan, are six similar constructions. A large blockhouse can also be found at Les Oblards, 800 yards due east of La Montagne.

Just outside Potijze village is Hussar Farm observation post, showing how buildings were used to produce and conceal

Hill 60 was eagerly sought and fiercely fought for by both sides. To the Germans the hill, made up of the spoil from the cutting from the railway running alongside it, gave domination over Ypres and the Salient. They built concrete bunkers and pill boxes to provide cover from British artillery, but these did not provide protection or cover from mining operations, and both sides were busy tunnelling. The British 23rd Division took over the front line from the 47th Division on 9 April, 1917. At 7pm that evening the Germans raided the newcomers, who, with the 1st Australian Tunnelling Company (there improving the mines driven by the Canadians for the attack on Messines Ridge), fended off the attackers. After the mine exploded on the morning of 7 June the Germans of the 204th Division in the bunkers and pill boxes were not in a condition to offer much resistance, and infantrymen of the Prince of Wales' Own West Yorkshires cleared the bunkers which had not been buried or destroyed. The British held the hill through the summer of 1917 and into the spring of 1918. In January and February, 1918, Hill 60, now on the corps defence line, was held by men of the 4th Australian Division. The 4th Field Company Australian Engineers, under Major J. H. Jolly, designed and built a pill box looking eastwards on top of an existing German bunker. An Australian machine-gun post was also sited in another pill box, the remains of which are 200 yards away. The position was given up to the Germans on the night of 15-16 April, 1918, with the British retiring to a line 400 yards to the west. The engineers' drawing was made to record and report construction details.

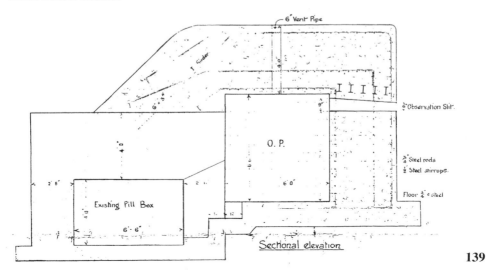

shell-proof structures. Hussar Farm was built in the same manner as Red House (see page 23), which stood until recent years a few hundred yards further west.

In the village of Zandvoorde is a 1916 German command post, still with its protective earth covering. The Pioneers who built it cast a plaque over the entrance. The bunker, with six chambers, has been cleared out by local volunteers. Between Zandvoorde and the British lines to the west lies Shrewsbury Forest, containing a number of German bunkers, some showing signs of being converted by the British. Hill 60, off the main road, has several remnants and an interesting pill box, built by the Australians over an original German bunker.

South of Hill 60, in the trees on the right of the road to Houthem just before the canal lock, is a concrete bunker with a heavy steel door still attached to its extension. Built as protection from British artillery sited behind the bluff beyond the trees, it gave enfilade fire on British troops working down through Battle Wood across the road. On the other side of the railway line to the east are some German bunkers built into the embankment. Command centres for the 204th Division, they were the British front line for the winter of 1917-1918 before being won back by the Germans. After being retaken they were used as divisional headquarters by the 34th Division in September, 1918.

On the left hand side of the N365, south out of Ypres, is Bedford House cemetery. In its centre are the remains of Rosendael Château, the cellars of which were fortified by the British. Further down on the same side of the road is a group of concrete shelters surrounded by a moat. Originally a moated farmhouse, Langhof Farm was an important centre to the British.

On down the N365 to St Eloi village and, in the angle of the junction with the N336, there are the remains of a German pill box built into the front line trench (Oaten Trench) facing the British in Crater Trench, 200 yards over the other side of the N365. Several yards away is a British bunker showing its corrugated iron sheet formwork. A short way along the N336, in a field on the left, is another British bunker. Built into Heile Farm which stood here, it served as protection for an officer and

Bedford House, discernible as a mound of rubble within the cemetery of that name, was originally called Rosendael Château. It, and its moats and surrounding land known as Bedford Camp, housed many British units after 1914. As part of the preparations for the attack on Messines Ridge planned for June, 1917, a brigade headquarters of the 47th (London) Division was based here. The 520th Field Company Royal Engineers was given the task of making the Château proof against German guns. On 25 January, 1917, a number of direct hits from 8.2" shells caused the brigade major to retire to the cellars when the bombardment interrupted his dinner. It was reported that the sweet course was unfinished. On 12 February, 1917, the sappers started work, using steel rails and girders to reinforce the concrete. The accommodation for eight officers and 100 men included brigade offices and mess, NCOs' and mens' cookhouse, and a signal office. During the battles of Messines the shell-proof cellars and surrounding grounds were always in occupation by one unit or other. In September, 1917, the Royal Welch Fusiliers stayed here, describing it as 'a smelly spot just south of Ypres'. In early 1918 it was turned into a strongpoint. On 27 April the 6th Battalion Leicester Regiment held off a major attack, although the Germans managed to reach within a few hundred yards of the site, midway between there and Langhof Farm just to the south. After that the Bedford House bunkers were held as a front line position by the 9th Battalion Norfolk Regiment. The cemetery was started by field ambulances which were based here. The concrete tops of some of the underground bunkers can still be seen in the rubble, although the entrances are all sealed off and buried.

" Bedford House", Ypres, 1917.

Langhof (sometimes Lankhof) Farm, originally a moated farm complex, was home to artillery and infantry units throughout the war. In the build-up to Messines, batteries of the 47th (London) Division were sited here from October, 1916. C/236 Battery Royal Field Artillery bombarded the Germans on Messines Ridge prior to the opening of the battle, and this 'Langhof Battery' provided support to the 23rd Division attempting to beat off a German attack at Hill 60 on 23 April, 1917. In November, 1917, as the Passchendaele fighting was grinding to a halt, it was decided to build shell-proof concrete shelters here. The 37th Division, resting there, and the Royal Engineers (153 Field Company) were given the task, under Major P. Moreton. On 21 November the Royal Engineers' divisional commander visited the site and 'decided to put in a small siding for stores for large concreting job here'. Early in January, 1918, the 4th Field Company Australian Engineers, 4th Australian Division, took the job over. In 1918 the British front line included Langhof. On 25 April, attempting to encircle and cut off Ypres, the German 7th Division, 18th Reserve Corps, pushed the British 21st Division back as far as Langhof. The bunkers were held by C Company, 6th Battalion, Leicesters, who spent 25 and 26 April improving the defences. At 9pm on 27 April a party of 250 Germans surrounded Langhof, forcing C Company to retire. A platoon from 8th Battalion were sent to recapture the bunkers, but were beaten off by machine-gun fire. D Company of the 7th Leicesters attacked at 3am on 28 April, but also failed. The bunkers today contain tiled fireplaces (made of tiles salvaged from the farmhouse ruins) as well as iron grates in some constructions.

twelve men of the Horse Artillery attached to the corps responsible for this sector.

Half a mile south of St Eloi, still on the N365, Onraet Wood holds a number of German bunkers, with another in the fields behind the wood. The 19th Western Division captured these from the German 2nd Division at the opening of the battle of Messines. The Germans retook them from the 1st Battalion East Yorkshire Regiment on 24 April, 1918.

Turning left, towards Hollebeke, 800 yards off the road as far as the right hand bend was the German front line. Three-quarters of a mile further on are the grounds of the (other) White Château, now a golf course. One hundred yards down the track to the left is a German bunker, preserved as part of the links. On Oak Support line, it was the scene of a determined attack by the 6th and 7th London Battalions of the 47th Division on 7 June, 1917. It was taken with the assistance of a tank and immediately turned into a strongpoint by the 520th Field Company Royal Engineers. During the winter the Australians held this sector and used German concrete blocks to build a new wall and doorway. The Australians wanted a better artillery observation post to overlook the other side of the canal, and built one into the ruins of the White Château itself. The 4th Field Company Australian Engineers, under Major Jolly, constructed it with reinforced concrete in the small copse there now. The earth covering the post is rubble from the Château.

In the fields around Oosttaverne Wood cemetery (once part of the woods) on the N336 are two German bunkers. On the southern edge of Oosttaverne behind a house on the right of the road is Polka Estaminet, a German bunker named after the building into which it was constructed. Made from pre-cast concrete blocks, it was part of the Oosttaverne Line, the objective of the 8th Lincolnshires on 7 June, 1917. Delays caused them to miss the start of the attack, so Polka Estaminet was taken by a company of the 52nd Australian Battalion under Captain Maxwell and later held as a front line post by the Border Regiment.

After a mile on the N336, just after crossing the Blaupoortbeek, 100 yards up the small road to the right is Delporte Farm, another German pill box. Further along the N336 and left at the next

Delporte Farm, built into a farmhouse of this name which stood here before the war, shows signs of the original building, retaining some of the internal brick walling in addition to the concrete block work. At 10pm on the night of 9 June, 1917, the 50th (South Australia) Battalion attacked Delporte Farm. Uncut wire and machine-gun fire caused the attack to fail. A second attempt the following night also failed, even following heavy bombardment and several direct hits on the pill box. On the night of 11 June the 50th Battalion and the 11th British Division took the pill box after close fighting. For some time this pill box marked the British front line.

crossroads, after 100 yards is a concrete gun emplacement on the left, the largest surviving on Messines Ridge. This emplacement (at the position 'the better 'ole' on trench maps) has heavy steel reinforcement and a concrete block outer skin. With the two pill boxes which stood in front, it was attacked by the 45th (New South Wales) Battalion, who took heavy casualties from machine-gun fire, as did the 49th (Queensland) Battalion who were trying to advance past it. It now houses cattle.

Picking up the N365 as it leaves Wytschaete in the direction of Messines, immediately to the right alongside a house is a squat, ivy-covered bunker named Pick House, with the entrance blocked by a wooden door.

Pick House, on the right of the N356 alongside the houses just south of Wytschaete (by the 3.5km marker) was the 36th (Ulster) Division's objective on 7 June, 1917, the opening of the battle of Messines. The bunker, housing a German battalion commander and his staff, was on the fourth (Black) line. The 10th Irish Rifles, having passed through the Red, Blue and Green lines, reached the bunker just after 7am. The garrison resisted strongly, but the Irishmen used a German machine-gun (the Allied Vickers gun crews, timed to arrive just after the 10th Irish Rifles to consolidate the line, had not yet reached the command bunker) to hold the position whilst bombers approached and bombed out the garrison, who then prudently decided to surrender. The Ulstermen's casualties were slight. Pick House then stayed in British hands for nearly a year. In April, 1918, the German advance caused the bunker to be fought over again. On 10 April, under the cover of a heavy morning mist, storm troops of the German 17th Reserve Division pushed the 10th Battalion Royal Warwickshires back to Pick House. The Warwickshires resisted to the best of their ability in defending and attempting to hold the position, but to no avail. Superior numbers on the attacking side forced them to retire. Shortly afterwards the South African Brigade developed a strong counterattack, in an attempt to retake the bunker, but this proved unsuccessful and Pick House was once again in German hands.

Still on the N365, passing through Messines the road bends to the left. On the right is the side road to the New Zealand Memorial Park, containing two pill boxes captured by the New Zealanders during the battle for Messines Ridge. The pill boxes, one of solid *in situ* concrete, the other of pre-cast concrete blocks, show the use of rear steps and a firing platform for the defenders. They demonstrate the protection given to the garrison, and have relatively minor damage from hits by artillery shells. One hundred yards away from the memorial car park, just over the road, are the remains of another pill box of the same group; another almost intact bunker is on the left of the Wulvergem road. About 500 yards south of the memorial park the roof of another concrete bunker, of different design, can be seen. Built by New Zealand Engineers, the front wall shows the effect of a direct hit from a large calibre shell, although the main structure is intact.

Continuing down the slope towards the French border, over the River Douve, lies Ploegsteert Wood, in which there are a number of concrete machine-gun emplacements, as they were known before the term pill box became widely used. They are strung out in a line in the wood behind the Keeper's Cottage, situated on the left of the road between the villages of Ploegsteert and Le Gheer on the southern edge of the wood. Close by is a first aid post with the name 'Blighty Hall' inscribed over the door. Benches for stretchers are still present, but, whilst the walls are fairly thick, the roof is thin, designed only to be proof against splinters and shrapnel. The remains of a similar bunker close by confirms that these structures were obviously not shell-proof.

Back to the N365, and on the left of the road on the west side of the wood (with the Ploegsteert Memorial to the Missing on the right) is an unusual three-chambered British bunker. Returning to the memorial and turning left just past it, at Hyde Park Corner, itself a British command post, there is Red Lodge, dug into the hill amongst the trees to the right, showing a roof with protuding steel reinforcing rails and an open rear. Past this post, along the second turning on the right, a British bunker with its original quarry-tiled floor intact has an unusual triangular observation window formed in its corner.

A similar construction, but with additional blast walls protecting

New Zealand Park stands on Uhlan Trench, 200 yards behind the German front line. The presence of the pill boxes standing here did not come as a surprise to the New Zealanders. They had watched the 40th (Saxon) Division constructing them in May, 1917. The 3rd New Zealand Rifle Brigade, who were to attack the position on 7 June, the opening day of the Messines offensive, said in an intelligence report on 7 May: 'Concrete work in two places, about 30 feet apart, appear to be dug-outs' and 'large dug-out with two or three layers of concrete bursters. Just behind the front line'. On 16 May one of the pill boxes was almost complete: 'Emplacement being worked on. Sheets of iron have taken place of camouflage materials previously seen'. Several bunkers along Uhlan Trench were observed to be under construction. At 3.10am on 7 June the New Zealanders attacked the position. Following a barrage and the eruption of a mine at Ontario Farm, 800 metres away, they stormed and took the bunkers with little difficulty. At 4.16am a report was received at the New Zealand headquarters that 'troops kept very close to barrage — enemy had no time to man his parapet'. Headquarters passed the report on, saying the first objectives of the attack were taken, and 'the infantry advanced to the attack — the attack was a magnificent success'. One bunker is of solid, in situ concrete, and one has outer layers of concrete blocks. Artillery hits are apparent. Loop-holes are not present, as a machine gun-fired over the top.

the entrance, is to be found behind Ploegsteert village on the right of the road heading towards Le Seau and the D933.

Little is left of the many bunkers built in 1917 and 1918 by the Australians, New Zealanders and British between Ploegsteert and Armentières. On the German side of this front several constructions remain, probably because a greater number existed. Along the D7 between Houplines and Pérenchies at the road junction known then, as now, as L'Aventure is an artillery observation post. Built into the café which stood on the corner, it still has the clay-tiled roof with steel ladder rungs to the top. At the base is the telephone bunker, which was connected to the gun battery nearby. Over the road is another bunker with observation ports (still with their wooden lining), looking over the front line towards the British 1,000 yards away.

A similar construction to L'Aventure, with signs of being built into the brick structure of a farm, is La Hutte Farm, on the left of the D36 between Funquereau and Croix-au-Bois. Standing high over the modern farmhouse, and with a protecting machine-gun pill box and command bunker beside it, the tall observation post gave good views into and beyond Armentiéres and British rear areas. The side road winding around the back of La Hutte Farm shows the British aspect of the post. Along this road, which eventually winds back to L'Aventure, there are a number of German bunkers in the fields and gardens of some of the houses.

The D36 southwards to Wez Macquart ran just behind the strongly defended German front line, which had been fairly static for most of the war. After passing a bunker by the junction of the back road to Houplines, two more can be found on the right just before the railway. The level crossing and approaches were protected by a machine-gun post, which can still be seen at the barn 200 yards to the left. Another, built into and jutting out of a farm building, is 500 yards further along on the left.

The front line, Incident Trench, crossed the D933 road 300 yards to the west of Wez Macquart. One mile east of the crossroads in the village lay the second main defence line, named Indeed Trench. Two pill boxes are on the right as the road bends slightly and starts to climb the rise. With machine-gun embrasures sweeping

La Hutte Farm observation post, near Funquereau on the D36, gave excellent views of the British front and rear areas in Armentières and Ploegsteert. Built into the farmhouse which stood here, the brick walls and concreted window openings are apparent and clearly indicate that the post gave observation at three heights. An artillery command bunker and protecting machine-gun pill box can also be found in this very interesting farmyard.

the road, they made any attack unlikely to succeed. Along this road about 100 yards before the junction with the D95 is a bunker under cover of trees just behind a roadside building. Around the crossroads at the junction itself is a cluster of bunkers. On the left by the new railway line is a covered concrete gun emplacement, which shielded a heavy gun firing on the British in front of and around Armentières. Just over the railway is another bunker, probably built as protection for the gunners. One hundred yards beyond the crossroads is a building (an old café) with a large square blockhouse built into its rear.

About two miles south-west of Bailleul, just before Outtersteene between the D23 and the railway, is Dermot House, a five-chambered bunker built into a fold of ground and the cellar of the adjacent farmhouse. Each chamber has an open rear and a forward facing concreted machine-gun emplacement (probably anti-aircraft defences). This is certainly one of the largest bunkers built by the British. It suffered severe damage in 1918 when it was taken by the Germans and then retaken by the British.

Dermot House, near Outtersteene, is a large British bunker with five separate compartments built into the cellars of the farmhouse which stood here in 1917. The area was relatively quiet, being about ten miles behind the front lines, although it was expected that the Germans would try to seize Hazebrouck and the rail centre in the spring of 1918. In April 1918 the Germans were rapidly approaching Dermot House, held by the 29th and 31st Divisions in turn. On 13 April the German 81st Regiment took it, and the bunker remained in their hands throughout the summer. The structure is one of the largest intact British bunkers on the Western Front.

Continuing on the D23, crossing the D947 at Vieux Berquin and on to the D188, on the left backing onto Aval Wood is La Rue de Bois British Cemetery. Opposite is a small farmhouse known to the British as Cobley Cottage, a field hospital. Jutting out from the rear of the barn is a large block-built bunker of the Arques (Second Army) pattern. The main doorway, inside the barn, has the date '22 Aug 1918' cast in large letters over the door.

Following the road to La Motte-au-Bois, turning left in the village along the D946 over the canal to the Forêt de Nieppe, then turning right on to the road that leads through the wood, several bunkers and pill boxes on both sides of the road dot the area where the British dug in after falling back in 1918. All are of the Aire (First Army) pattern, with the distinctive marks of the blocks and beams of this factory. Three block-built pill boxes are just inside the southern edge of the wood, off the road between Merville and Haverskerque. In perfect condition, they were constructed in July, 1918, by the 250 Tunnelling Company (5th Division). On the right of the D946 towards Merville, just inside the easterly point of the wood, are the remains of Les Lauriers pill box, started in July, 1918, by the 257 Tunnelling Company.

Turning left off the D916 along the by-road to Merville, just before crossing the canal there is a concrete block pill box guarding the canal bank behind St Floris. A corner is missing due to a German shell, and shows the loose-laid block construction, highlighting how the blocks moved when hit. Later constructions had the blocks cemented together. A similar pattern bunker stands in a field 200 yards north of the Merville road; several others — from the same defence line — can be found around the hamlet of Les Amuzoire, on the small road from St Floris to Robecq.

The Royal Engineers were busy in this area during 1918. One construction of the 66th Divisional Engineers is on the left of the D937 just before Hinges. It formed part of the Mont Bernanchon defences (see page 107).

Just over a mile on the right along the N42 west of Hazebrouck is Les Cinq Rues Military Cemetery. Outside, towards the railway, is a Moir pill box built as part of the West Hazebrouck Line in 1918. Standing well up from ground level, unusual for a pre-cast pill box of this type, it has a second external layer of concrete to

Nieppe Forest and the surrounding villages became important British military centres in 1918, as the Germans approached and stopped on the eastern edge of the wood. St Floris, held by the 61st Division at the bridgehead south of the wood, was just behind the front line, and the Royal Engineers attached to the division spent the summer of 1918 constructing defences in the area, including many pill boxes. The sappers of 250 Tunnelling Company assisted them and built a number of concrete pill boxes of the First Army pattern from the Aire-sur-la-Lys factory. The site for each was chosen by the Machine Gun Battalion in accordance with corps plans. After construction, each was handed over to a field company who were responsible for final completion, fitting gas curtains and gun mountings, any additional camouflage, and clearing the field of fire. Several can still be visited and inspected. Over the canal from St Floris, on the right a few hundred yards from the D916 road bridge, is a concrete block pill box built by 250 Tunnelling Company and manned by the Gordon Highlanders and other battalions of the 61st Division. Sited to cover any German approach along the canal, it took a hit from a shell on the rear corner, showing up a fault in the construction. The blocks are held together with steel reinforcing bars but not cemented together, and therefore more likely to suffer major damage from a direct hit. Three identical pill boxes, also built by 250 Company, are just inside the forest behind Le Corbie hamlet off the D122. Other bunkers, all built from the same type of blocks but with different layouts, can be found in the forest on either side of the Haverskerque-Le Préavin road.

increase the overall thickness. The West Hazebrouck Line continues over the N42, heading south on the small road, and on the right at the approach to the first crossroads stands a large British pill box of the Arques (Second Army) pattern No. 3 design. About 200 yards south is a Moir pill box, built by the same Royal Engineers company in the ruined farmhouse which stood there.

Following the road southwards, turn left on the D138 towards Morbecque and, about half a mile on the right is a British command bunker with two protected entrances sheltering in the dead ground behind the hill. A standard design from the Arques factory, with rear-facing doorways and a strong roof, it was one of many in this section of the GHQ Line.

South of Armentières the D22 runs to Bois Grenier, and along this roadside are some square, German forward pill boxes with the dates '30/4/17' and '4/17' cast into their concrete.

The West Hazebrouck Line was one of the last defence lines constructed by the British in 1918. Many pill boxes were built in the area south of the N42. At Les Six Rues, a small road on the right of the D238 north of La Belle Hôtesse, is a pill box built to the GHQ standard specification. Designed to be sited in pairs for mutual cover, and to take two Vickers machine-guns, it had a wide field of fire. This pattern had a buried one-inch pipe laid from 1,000 yards behind for conveying compressed air. In a bombardment, and when machine-guns were in use, fresh air was to be pumped in. If the enemy captured it, gas could be pumped in. This pill box is the only one of this type surviving. It was built in late August 1918, making it one of the very last pill boxes built by either side in the war. Its general design influenced the shape of pill boxes built in Britain in the 1940s.

From Fleurbaix the D171 winds down and follows just behind the line of the British front. A mile after leaving Fleurbaix, on the right just after the crossroads and before the sharp bend in the road, a reinforced concrete shelter, built by the 505 (Wessex) Field Company for the 57th Division in January, 1918, sits in the garden of a modern house. Further down the Dl71 at Pétillon, on the same side of the road, is a British concrete bunker. It has little strength and is most unlikely to have withstood a direct hit or to have given much protection to its inhabitants.

The British front line ran along the flat plain, with the Germans dug in on the slopes of Aubers Ridge above them. They occupied this high ground throughout the war. In and around the villages between Bois Grenier and La Bassée are ninety-six pill boxes, bunkers and observation posts. Some bear the constructors' details or completion dates, and many were concealed by being built into existing buildings.

The village of Le Maisnil (Le Mesnil), with Somerset Farm observation post behind it, held sway over the British in the wet land below, as did Aubers. In the centre of the latter village is an artillery command centre and observation tower, also a *Blinkstelle* (light-signalling station) sending messages which were relayed back to Wavrin. A plaque on the tower reads *'Beobachtungsturm Erbaut 1916 von der Bay. Res. Pion. Komp. 7'*.

Just outside Illies, at Bouchaine, is an observation post, a group of bunkers and a command post, obviously an artillery site. In the flat land fronting the Aubers Ridge stand many front and second line pill boxes. Those at Pietre were built at trench level. Butt House, a chambered concreted barn up the track to the right off the D41 towards Fauquissart, is built above ground, just behind the front line within view of the British. The Bois de Biez, between Lorgies and Neuve Chapelle, has a German bunker on its southern tip with inscriptions on the wall of the right chamber. *'Gott Mit Uns'* and a clock have survived the damp conditions.

The most southerly of these constructions facing Aubers Ridge are near Le Transloy and La Bassée, between the D41 and D947, behind Violanes, the German front line village. Between La Bassée and Béthune lay the British front line villages of Festubert and Givenchy. Along the D166, in Festubert, is a large

Somerset Farm, east of Le Mesnil, is situated just behind the crest of Aubers Ridge. Known as Amberg 1 by the Germans, the farm was a divisional artillery headquarters post. The tower overlooked the British lines, but was screened from British observation by trees and the buildings in Le Mesnil. In addition to the existing tower, there were officers' quarters, a light-signalling station, and four bunkers, all built in strong, shell-proof concrete. Viewed from the air or the ground there was little to indicate the importance and extensive nature of the constructions. Somerset Farm was captured by the 47th (London) Division on 3 October, 1918, and photographed as part of the report on the defence system.

Tramways House, Festubert, featured in the fighting and defence of Festubert and Givenchy by the 55th Division in April, 1918. The village had been occupied by the 42nd Division up to February, 1918, and Royal Engineers companies were very active in constructing concrete shelters in December, 1917, and January, 1918. 427 Field Company were very busy building shelters here, describing them as 'ferro-concrete shelters in the third line of defence, known as the Village Line. These shelters were made by placing together heavy corrugated-iron sheets bent to the shape of part of a circle and bolted together in the rooms of the houses, and building over them walls three feet thick and roof four feet thick of ferro-concrete.' Shortages of materials and labour prevented more shelters from being started, but 427 Company were pleased with their work: 'The few that were completed were found to be 5.9" shell-proof and materially helped the 55th Division three months later to make their famous stand against the big German offensive.' On 9 April, 1918, the British front line was east of Festubert; the Village Line was the houses along Festubert road, down through Le Plantin to the canal. The village was in the 165 Brigade sector, with several battalions of the King's Liverpool Regiment in residence. At 4.15am on 9 April the Germans laid down a heavy bombardment of explosives and gas. Men of the 1/7th and 1/6th Liverpools sat out the bombardment in Tramways House. The shelling continued for the next two days, with German infantry of the 43rd Reserve Division attacking and taking the front line, coming close to the bunker. On 10 April an attack between 1.30pm and 3pm was beaten back. The Germans tried again the following day, capturing a strongpoint just in front of the bunker. A party of Liverpudlians led by Major Keet reoccupied the point soon after. The front line remained close to Tramways House for the rest of the summer, but was pushed back after an attack by units of the 55th Division in late September, 1918. The brickwork and structure of the original house can be seen, incorporated into the concrete walls. Tramways House was inhabited until the 1970s.

double-roomed bunker built into a house which stood there. Probably constructed in December, 1917, by the Royal Engineers and infantry of the 42nd East Lancashire Division, alongside the terminal of a light railway, it was part of the Village Line defences. It was used as headquarters by the 1/7th King's Liverpool Regiment when the Germans attacked Festubert on 9 April, 1918. The bunker was held for two days under heavy bombardment, which destroyed most of the village. In the afternoon of 11 April the German 43rd Reserve Division, just back from Russia, attacked and managed to get within 500 yards of it before being beaten back by the Liverpudlians. A British pill box, with a machine-gun embrasure and brickwork patterns from being cast into a brick building, is in the back garden of a house nearby.

After the April fighting the 55th Division built more concrete shelters in the wooded marshes behind Festubert. In the middle of these woods (take the side road west out of the village and turn left at the first junction), dotted around a group of houses, are seven bunkers built in the summer of 1918, most bearing the Lancashire Rose, the divisional sign of the East Lancashires. Another bunker, King's Post, can be found by returning to the junction and taking the next left.

In the marshy woods behind Festubert are shelters constructed by Royal Engineers of the 55th (West Lancashire) Division, following their battle which stopped the German advance on this front in April, 1918. All the shelters bear the crest of the Red Rose, the emblem of Lancashire and the 55th Division. One group contains seven bunkers, all built by 419 Field Company in June, 1918. King's Post stands on its own, a large bunker designed as a brigade headquarters. Next to the Red Rose emblem by the door is the imprint of the Royal Engineers. The bunker was probably given the name of King's Post after the King's (Liverpool) Regiment, which had six battalions in the division.

An example of a standard circular-pattern pill box built of brick with a reinforced concrete roof can be found just inside the north-west corner of Gorre Wood. This model is identical to two covering the approach to the Canal de la Lawe and sited in the small road on the left of the D171. Constructed by 145 Army Troops Company Royal Engineers in the autumn of 1917, these pill boxes were manned by the 2nd Royal Scots and 1st Royal Scots Fusiliers on 11 April, 1918, when the 1st Bavarian Reserve Division attacked from the north-east. The following day the Germans captured Locon, and the pill boxes were within 1,000 yards of the front line.

Other defensive positions were built by various divisions in the second and third lines of this sector. In 1918 the British adopted many patterns of concrete machine-gun emplacement. A standard circular pattern, built of brick with a reinforced concrete roof, was used to produce a defence line around Béthune. It ran in front of the town, near the villages of Hinges, Les Choquaux, Essars, Gorre, Le Quesnoy and Beuvry, and was named Hamel Switch, part of the 1st Corps Defences. Two emplacements are behind a farm on a small road to the left of the D171, a mile and a half after its junction with the D945. These covered the approach to the Canal de la Lawe and were designed to be 5.9" shell-proof, although the brickwork had limitations in withstanding high explosives. They were erected in the autumn of 1917 by 145 Army Troops Company Royal Engineers, who described them as 'brick and concrete circular machine-gun emplacements — the type now to erect'. Another example is just inside the north-west corner of Gorre Wood, defending the Lawe canal behind Le Hamel.

In a bend of the D72 east of Gorre is another shelter, probably built by the 42nd Division and used by the Lancashire Fusiliers as headquarters at the opening of the German offensive on 9 April, 1918.

The triangle formed by the towns of Béthune, Douai and Arras, with Lens in its centre, played an important part in the war and was bitterly contested, being heavily industrial and densely populated. At the crossroads of Le Rutoire, north of Loos, is a British pill box in the grounds of a farmhouse. A German gun emplacement is off the side road in the angle formed by the D947 and the A21, and a tall observation post, built into the tower which stood here, can be found by turning off the N17 into Annay. The railhead and canal betwen Pont-à-Vendin and Vendin-le-Vieil was a major bridgehead and defensive zone for the Germans.

To the north of Arras, in the Souchez valley between the D937 and Givenchy-en-Gohelle, stand the remains of British experiments to assess the effects of artillery fire on various types of concrete walls.

The villages on the eastern side of Vimy Ridge, such as Farbus and Willerval, were German administrative and command centres harbouring bunkers and shelters built into houses and gardens.

To the east of Arras was the hinge of the German withdrawal to the Hindenburg Line, or *Siegfriedstellung*. Whilst this name was given to the continuous front line trench, it was in fact a series of positions with other defence lines (the Sailly-Proville line, the Masnières-Fonsomme line, the Drocourt-Quéant line, and so on) provided for the Germans to fall back on if necessary. Effective defences were developed, with carefully sited pill boxes, observation posts, gun emplacements, shelters and tunnels. Those north of the N44/D917 junction at Bonavis were used during the battles of Arras and Cambrai in 1917. Those south of Bonavis were successful in preventing British advances until March, 1918. The defences and fortifications were used again in September and October, 1918, when the Germans fell back, but the troops were in disarray and unable to use them to their best advantage.

West of the N17 is the Somme area fought over in 1916, when the British and French attempted to push back the Germans.

In the Souchez valley, to the north-east of Souchez village, stand three concrete monoliths built to test the effect of a direct hit from an 18-pound shell fired at very close range. The test pieces were constructed in October and November, 1917, by 230 Army Troops Company, Royal Engineers. The tests were carried out on 18 December, 1917, in the presence of senior army officers, to assess the strengths of various types of in situ and pre-cast systems. The tests were fully reported and analysed, and the information gained from them affected British design and construction in 1918. The Souchez valley had been held by the French until March, 1916. It was out of the sight of German artillery observation (the front line trenches were just below the ridge, approximately where the motorway is today), although it was continuously shelled as the Germans knew that British artillery sheltered here. A particularly heavy bombardment filled the valley on 21 May, 1916, in advance of a German attempt to push the British off the ridge and down into the valley. Battalions of the London Regiment suffered heavy casualties in their fight to hold on to the slopes and ridge. Several British counterattacks were made and beaten off. At 2am on 22 May the 15th London (Civil Service Rifles) and others made a determined effort to hold the position, but were almost annihilated. The order to hold the front line cost sixty-three officers and 2,044 other ranks in casualties, of whom 910 were killed. The Germans held the top of the ridge until being pushed back by the 38th (Ottawa) and 78th (Winniepeg Grenadiers) Battalions of the 4th Canadian Division on 9 April, 1917.

Just off the D929 Bapaume-Albert road (bisecting the 1916 battlefield), going towards Grévillers, is a large bunker. Although typically German, its position in the lee of the high ground and the direction it faces suggests it may be British, dating from after the German withdrawal.

Continuing through Grévillers along the D29 (which becomes the D163) on through Irles, the road reaches the village of Miraumont, given up by the German 18th Division when it pulled back to the Hindenburg Line in March, 1917. Heading towards Achiet on the D50, in the embankment is the concrete and brick entrance to an underground bunker, fought for on 24 August, 1918, when the Germans resisted the 42nd and 21st Divisions. Further down the Ancre valley the high ground to the north-east of Beaucourt-sur-l'Ancre has a German shell-proof observation post overlooking the valley. Defended by the German 38th Division, it was taken by the Royal Naval Division on 13 November, 1916. Another German post, the Schwaben Redoubt on the edge of Thiepval, can be seen from here. Opposite Thiepval Wood, from where the 36th (Ulster) Division attacked on 1 July, 1916, are the remains of an observation post (identified by the upright steel rails reinforcement) close to the German front line.

Pozières has an observation post called Gibraltar, still with stairs leading down to its bunker. From Pozières a small track leads to Martinpuich, where a round-topped German bunker sits in the trees. At the junction of several light railways, a large dump and stores, it was held by the 17th and 23rd Regiments, 3rd (Bavarian) Division, and captured by units of the 15th Division on 15 September, 1916.

In a field off a back street in Guillemont are several concrete dug-outs with blocked entrances. The D20 from Guillemont to Combles passes Bouleux and Leuze Woods on the left and right respectively. In the south-west corner of Leuze Wood is a concrete observation post. Credit for its capture was given to the Devonshire Regiment, 5th Division, although the 7th Inniskillings lay claim to the honour. In Combles, behind a warehouse on the north-east edge of the village, is a German bunker wrested from the 52nd (Reserve) Division by the 56th (London) Division.

Just outside Thiepval, 120 yards down the track branching off in front of the Ulster Tower, is a reinforced concrete observation post (identified by the upward jutting steel reinforcing beams), which sat on the German front line on 1 July, 1916. Built 300 yards from the British front line, its entrance at trench level gave sufficient shelter for a man to watch the British in their lines in the trees opposite. The German front line was heavily bombarded prior to the attack on 1 July, 1916, but although the wire was demolished, this strong concrete post survived undamaged. An observer of the German 99th Regiment in the bunker would have seen waves of Ulstermen of the Royal Irish Rifles leaving the cover of the woods at 7.15am to attack the front line (which was taken at 7.30am) before passing on to capture the Schwaben Redoubt on the high ground behind. The Ulstermen were held up by machine-gun fire from Thiepval village and the northern side of the Ancre, but managed to hold on to the post and surrounding trench. At 4.00pm the West Yorkshire Regiment tried to reinforce them, but were cut down by machine-gun fire between the wood and the observation post. At 9.00pm another attempt was made, and this time the West Yorkshires met with the remnants of the Ulstermen and held on at the Schwaben Redoubt until forced out by a German counterattack. The observation post, at that time without any damage, was sheltered from the German artillery and remained in the forward part of the British line for another three months, until the Germans were pushed off the high ground of Thiepval Ridge and village. In the spring of 1918 the post was again the scene of much action: on 25 March the remains of Drake and Howe Battalions of the 63rd (Royal Naval) Division made a stand here against the advancing Germans. Drake recorded that 'we withdrew in a masterly fashion to Thiepval',[35] where the 4th Bedfords joined them, losing two officers before crossing the Ancre on the following day, 26 March. The observation post was then reoccupied by the Germans, who crossed the Ancre before being forced to stop their advance. The post was recaptured by the 6th Leicesters when they attacked on 22 August, 1918.

162

In Chilly, south-west of Chaulnes, a pill box shows impressions of the brick walls against which the concrete was cast. Overlooking the French first line in 1916, it was used on 10 August, 1918, against the 12th Canadian Brigade.

East along the D39 to Hallu is an infantry strongpoint, open at two ends and with rifle apertures. The Canadian 78th Battalion took it on 10 August, 1918, and lost it again the next day. It was retaken the same day by the 50th Battalion.

The double-chambered concrete bunker on the south-west edge of Martinpuich village (in an orchard off the Bazentin-le-Petit road) was at the junction and siding of a light railway in a large German dump and stores area. Held by the 17th Bavarian Regiment, it was captured by Scotsmen of the 15th Division at first light on 15 September, 1916, making this one of the earliest examples of German reinforced concrete constructions taken by the British. The Scotsmen who captured the bunker were to have been assisted by four tanks; only one arrived, but it helped the attack and crushed some dug-outs before returning for petrol. The bunker shows the results of a number of hits from British shells on one side. Some of the damage is not severe, which shows the effectiveness of the shelter in providing protection.

Baizieux Tower, on the ridge of a gentle rise on the Hénencourt-Baizieux road, had a concrete machine-gun emplacement porthole built into the lower part of its thick masonry walls in the summer of 1918. The field of fire for the post made it a good position on Moon Trench, although it was eventually not used as the Germans did not advance beyond Albert.

In and around the villages west and north of Albert are pill boxes and bunkers dating from the summer of 1918, when the British were constructing defences after being pushed back by the Germans. Having stopped them on the edge of Albert, the British ensured their defences were sufficient to ward off other attacks. The road westward from Hénencourt Château towards Baizieux rises, and by the crossroads at the top is the tower of an old windmill which the British converted to a concrete reinforced machine-gun emplacement.

To guard against a German advance along the Albert-Amiens road the Australians built the Lahoussoye Line around the village of that name. It included several pill boxes behind the village, three of which are in fields between Lahoussoye and the D78. Another is on the western edge. (see page 104) An observation post, also Australian built, looks over and along the Ancre and Somme valleys, from the ridge south of the D30 between Corbie and Pont Noyelles.

In the road bank in Coisy, overlooking the ground falling away down into Amiens, is a Moir pill box which formed part of the the GHQ Line. It still has its revolving steel bullet-proof protecting ring and Vickers machine-gun bracket. In Hérissart village the lower half of a Moir pill box is used as a cattle trough. A trench system, the Purple Line, ran north of Albert through Colincamps

In Hénencourt village there are eight pill boxes dating from the summer of 1918. The village, with its imposing château, had been a quiet rear area in 1916 and 1917. In late March, 1918, the Germans had advanced to as near as Albert, two and a half miles away, and the village streets were teeming with weary troops of the 17th Division. The village was later fortified in case of further German advances. The 47th (London) Division was based here from the end of April, and Royal Engineers of the division completed a trenching and wiring scheme (started by the 12th Division) before the construction of concrete pill boxes. The handing over of the area from one company of engineers to another was not a smooth affair. Sappers of the 47th Division reported that their predecessors 'were most disagreeable people to have dealings with'. Lieutenant P. H. Wakefield and troops of 520 Field Company, with infantry working parties from the London Regiment, spent most of July and early August constructing shell-proof emplacements for Vickers and Lewis gun posts around the village. These posts covered the approaches from the north-east, east, south and south-west of the village, and were manned by divisional machine-gun crews. Later work was assisted by one officer and fourteen NCOs and men of the 108th Engineer Regiment of the 33rd American Division, who were attached for instruction. Work continued until 10 August, 1918, two days after the successful British offensive. This half-completed pill box is on the south-west edge of Hénencourt, and stands about six feet high in a field down a track off the Bresle road. A second is on the edge of the village on the Laviéville road, with another about 200 yards away beside a house on the other side of the road. This was built inside a café which stood here. The fourth pill box in this group is on the right as the Senlis road leaves the village. The defence scheme included the château. Built into its perimeter wall, on the D91 road to Warloy-Daillon, is a large pill box with apertures overlooking the fields opposite. Beside this pill box, about thirty yards along and behind the masonry wall, is another with apertures cut into the lower brickwork. This structure is unusual in that it still contains the mounting with spigot for a Vickers machine gun. Not a standard Vickers mounting, this was apparently especially fabricated to be fitted in situ with the pill box. A standard Vickers mounting can be found in the pill box built into the eastern perimeter wall (150 yards from the limestone corner tower on the Senlis road). This pill box was built into the château orangery, and still contains the gardeners' access stairs.

and Sailly-au-Bois to Gommecourt. An old barn on the left of the D23 from Colincamps to Sailly-au-Bois has a pill box and observation post in it. Its blocked apertures can be seen from the outside, as can the marks of small-arms fire in the brickwork. (see page 109) In a field south-west of Sailly-au-Bois, off the track on the right of the Courcelles road, is a concrete pill box, identical to the one north of Hébuterne, facing Gommecourt Park on the British front line of 1 July, 1916.

Other examples of this pattern still exist by the D62 between Berles-au-Bois and Bienvillers-au-Bois; the roof of one is in a field on the left on leaving the village, and another, also on the left, a mile and a half along the road. Also between these villages, 200 yards from the road, is a machine-gun emplacement with walls of brickwork and rubble six feet thick. The position covers the valley and any approach from the east. Monchy-au-Bois was the front line for the Germans and was strongly defended. To the south is the high ground named Chemin des Dames by the British, who built a concrete machine-gun post here in 1918. It is 300 yards from the D3 Foncquevillers road, on the crest of the high ground looking east. Just behind the 1916 German front line (reached by taking the track to the left on arriving at the village on the D3) is the remains of a 1916 German observation post.

A 1918 British observation post, looking towards the German front line to the north of Adinfer Wood, is by the track running parallel to the D3 between Monchy-au-Bois and Ransart. Just inside the southern perimeter of Adinfer Wood, by the road from Douchy-les-Ayette, is a large German artillery observation and command bunker; still with remnants of large Gothic script cast into the outer wall, and a 1918 Royal Engineers inscription inside. The post commanded fire for several German heavy batteries during the 1916 battles on the Somme. Visitors should note that entry to the wood is forbidden.

In Rossignol Wood, left of the D6 Gommecourt-Puisieux road, are the remains of a bunker, probably an early German one built before July, 1916. In the trees along the road between Blaireville and the D3 are the remnants of a British observation post from the summer of 1918, probably constructed by the Guards Division.

Hébuterne was twice behind the British front line, once in 1916 and again after March, 1918. A pill box on the edge of the village, on the right of the D28 road to Fonquevillers, faces the trees of Gommecourt Park, which was the German front line in 1916. The pill box is on the site of the British front line trench of 1 July, 1916, when men of the London Rifle Brigade walked towards the machine-guns as part of a diversionary attack to prevent the German 55th Regiment from assisting their comrades further south. This pill box was not there at that time. On 28 March, 1918, a mixed force of Australians and New Zealanders prevented the 3rd Guards Regiment of the German 14th Reserve Corps from entering Hébuterne. The 1916 front line position then became a section of the Purple System, a second defence line which included Gommecourt, Hébuterne and Sailly-au-Bois. Over the next months the British were active in constructing strong defences, including many pill boxes, along this line. Some Moir pill boxes were erected, but most were a simple design of an in situ concrete machine-gun emplaceent over a dug-ut. The 42nd (East Lancashire) Division held this sector from April to June, 1918, and constructed pill boxes of in situ *and pre-cast types. Royal Engineers of the division (427, 428 and 429 Companies) sited and started the works, helped by Pioneers of the 307th Regiment of the American 77th Division, who were attached for training. In June the New Zealanders took over the sector and completed the works. They manned the pill box at O'Briens Post, which still stands. It was active in providing cover to infantry and firing upon German patrols. An identical pill box, also part of the Purple System and finished and manned by the New Zealanders, is down a track to the south-west of Sailly-au-Bois. The photographs show the pill boxes opposite Gommecourt Wood (top) and Sailly-au-Bois (below). Other examples of the same pattern are to be found at Coigneux (near Rossignol Farm, by the track to Bayencourt), and to the north of the D6 between Souastre and Foncquevillers. Some 150 yards away from the latter is the concrete roof of a large subterranean British command bunker, probably a divisional headquarters.

All over the area that was the Western Front, other pill boxes and bunkers can be found in fields, villages and barns. Of the many thousands built by both sides in the First World War, they remain as mute witnesses to the conditions which made them necessary.

24 *The Wet Flanders Plain* by Henry Williamson (Faber & Faber, 1929).
25 *The Pill Boxes of Flanders* by Colonel E. G. L. Thurlow (British Legion, 1933).
26 *Twenty Years After, The Battlefields of 1914-18: Then and Now* edited by Major-General Sir Ernest Swinton (George Newman Ltd, London 1938).
27 *I Was There* edited by Sir John Hammerton (Amalgamated Press, London 1939).
28 *Ieper en de frontstreek* by Caenepeel and Annoot (Uitgeverig AG.).
29 *Storm of Steel* by Ernst Junger (Chatto and Windus).
30 *In the Cannon's Mouth* by P. J. Cambell (Hamish Hamilton).
31 *Some Desperate Glory* by Edwin Campion Vaughan (Leo Cooper, London 1981).
32 *War Diary* 4 October, 1917, 40th Battalion, Australian Imperial Forces.
33 *Report on Operations* by Captain F. Chesnutt-Chesney.
34 *The History of the Royal Irish Rifles* by C. Falls (Gale and Polden, 1925).
35 *War Diary*, Drake Battalion, 63rd (Royal Naval) Division.

GLOSSARY

Many terms used in fortification engineering and design have evolved over many hundreds of years of European castle and fort construction; words such as *banquette*, *batardeau*, *orillon*, *tenaille* and *terreplein* have specific meanings and convey much to the military engineer. Many experienced Royal Engineers maintained the correct use of terms; equally, however, numerous words had their meanings altered by misuse. Many words were interchangeable in general use: for example, bunker, blockhouse and pill box (and sometimes dug-out) may have been used to describe the same structure. For the purposes of this book the 1914-1918 meanings have been used, with the same lack of precision. The listed engineering terminology was in general use.

abri   A general French term for shelter: in military usage, shelter from artillery fire.

blockhouse   A term for a strong building or sheltered part of a barracks. In the war the term became widely used to describe shell-proof cover, and was interchangeable with *bunker* and *pill box*.

MEBU   (Mannschafts-Eisen-Beton-Unterstand)   An abbreviation commonly used by the Germans, meaning literally a reinforced concrete shelter for troops to stand under. Also used by the British, until *pill box* became more common.

dead ground   The safe area behind a hill, out of sight of artillery observation. Not to be confused with *killing ground*.

dug-out   A chamber dug into the earth to shelter from the elements and artillery fire, sometimes used for ground level or above ground shelters. Also used to describe a retired officer recalled for active service.

embrasure   The lower part of a crenellation, through which men or artillery could fire. In trench warfare the term was used for a cut-away section of the parapet. In *pill boxes*, a hole for a machine gun to be fired through.

fascine A cylindrical bundle of timber, sometimes filled with earth, widely used in trench warfare to strengthen trenches and increase the height of the parapet. Also used to describe a flat sheet of wickerwork sticks, again used for trench support.

flank side Used to denote the side of a body of troops. To outflank was to pass to the side of the enemy and gain a strategic advantage.

in situ In place or in position. In concrete work, to be cast into permanent position.

killing ground An area designed to be exposed to machine-gun or artillery fire, usually formed by strategic design of barbed wire layout.

monolith A single stone or piece, used for a large mass of concrete.

pill box A term properly used for a shell-proof concrete machine-gun emplacement, but used generally to describe any concrete shelter or protection.

pre-cast A method of making concrete blocks and beams for transportation and use elsewhere.

rampart A bank of earth used to provide a defensive cover for troops or artillery.

redoubt A small, detached, independent manned position with fire cover to front and sides.

salient A line of defence which juts out into the enemy's line and can give and receive fire from front and sides.

Stellung German for position or trench line; used for either a single trench or a trench system.

strongpoint An independent position, or section of trench line, capable of providing fire on all sides and strong enough to prevent enemy intrusion or passage.

Appendix I

Report: GERMAN STRUCTURES ON MESSINES RIDGE AND EFFECT OF SHELL FIRE ON THEM

Appendix II

Report: GERMAN STRUCTURES NORTH OF YPRES AND EFFECT OF SHELL FIRE ON THEM

Appendix III

USE OF FERRO-CONCRETE IN DUG-OUT CONSTRUCTION

APPENDIX I

E. in C. Fieldwork
Notes No. 31.

GERMAN CONCRETE STRUCTURES ON MESSINES RIDGE AND THE EFFECT OF SHELL FIRE ON THEM.

(From reports : 105th Field Coy., R.E.; 250th Tunnelling Coy., R.E.; 9th Field Coy., Australian Engineers ; 12th Field Coy., Australian Engineers; 3rd Australian Pioneer Battn.; 4th Australian Pioneer Battn., etc.)

The nature of the ground on Messines Ridge, where there is water bearing sand about 20 feet below the surface, made the construction of deep dug-outs there impossible. The mined dug-outs that have been found have only 10 to 15 feet of earth cover. For the protection of his men from shell fire the enemy resorted largely to concrete shelters. The roofs of these shelters were originally about, or just about, surface level, but shell fire has exposed considerable portions of them, so that they now stand out above ground more than the designers intended. A variety of types are to be found. By the aid of these and the official manuals the gradual development of German concrete construction can be traced.

Two methods of construction have been employed :—

    (*a*) Monolithic ferro-concrete, and

    (*b*) Ferro-concrete blocks.

From the beginning ferro-concrete was used in preference to plain concrete ; but at first the reinforcement was not scientifically applied. Steel joists and rails were usually employed. Failing these, iron screw pickets, hoop iron, angle iron pickets and scraps of iron were thrown in. The regular form of construction was discarded apparently in consequence of the weakness of the bond between joists and rails and the concrete. Further, where close girders were employed for roof support, " in nearly all cases heavy shells have moved the roofs bodily although there are very few entirely destroyed."—(105th Field Company.)

Another explanation of the failure of joist and rail reinforcement is possibly furnished by the French experiences at Verdun. There the dislocation and cracking of ferro-concrete under heavy shell fire was attributed to the difference in intensity and velocity of the vibrations in the iron and the concrete, which occasioned a separation of the two materials. It may be that the vibrations in girders and rails have a more disturbing effect on the mass of the concrete than the vibrations in rods. At any rate in the German Manual of the Construction of Field Positions (Stellungsbau), in both editions (June 1916 and December 1916), it is laid down that joists and rails are not to be used if round iron rods are available.

In the *first form of reinforcement by round iron*, a frame work of rods *uniformly distributed* over the whole structure was employed. Both in plan and section the cross rods formed a series of squares, see Plate 1. The reinforcements illustrated in " Stellungsbau " edition of December, 1916, show this pattern alone.

In the *latest form* (*see* Plates 2 and 3) there are in the roof several layers of reinforcement near the surface, and one layer close to the bottom of the concrete. In the centre there is occasionally another layer, but as a rule none. Thus the *reinforcement is principally near the surface.* Construction is of course much facilitated by the reduction in the amount of iron ; an unbroken mass of concrete is provided, which is not liable to be dislocated by vibration of iron in it ; the surface is given tensile strength.

The side walls are sometimes built in similar fashion, sometimes there is only one ladder of reinforcement on each surface.

The *reports* show that reinforced concrete structures of this nature will resist shell fire :—

    " Nearly all the dug-outs (Fig. 2)—(twelve seen)—have had direct hits. The effect of shell fire was practically nil, and in no case had it affected the concrete lower than the second row of reinforcement."—(9th Field Co., Australian Engineers.)

    " Direct hits from shells had very little damaging effect. The outer skin of reinforcing seems to be the secret. I actually saw a direct hit, I think a 5·9 in.; the reinforcement was only penetrated to the extent of 4 in. Some of the shelters received as many as seven direct hits."—(9th Field Co., Australian Engineers.)

    " In no case did damage extend beyond actual concrete blown away. Reinforcing iron was undamaged."—(105th Field Co., R.E.)

    " The combination of reinforcement and mass has been so successfully worked out that some of the structures have been knocked out of plumb without cracking. . . . The typical single chamber dug-out could not have been in a more exposed position. The ground around is a mass of interlocking shell holes and yet no concrete is destroyed beyond the layer of steel bar reinforcement. . . . From the proportion of void to solid in the section it can be seen that for the purposes of destruction the shelter must be considered a solid block of reinforced concrete."—

                                           (12th Field Co., Australian Engineers.)

1

The effect of shell fire on mass concrete as observed in our lines is :-

(a) To cause it to fail in tension.

This is avoided in enemy dug-outs by bottom reinforcement, which also serves to prevent heavy pieces of concrete falling into the casemate, if the mass is injured.

(b) To cause it to crack and star like glass. This is avoided in these dug-outs by the use of heavy top and sometimes central ladder reinforcement. " It is probable that this exterior reinforcement is unnecessarily heavy ; and that two layers of X.P.M. 8-in. mesh, $\frac{3}{8}$-in. by $\frac{1}{8}$-in. gauge, with shear stirrups would be equally effective and much more easy to place."

The inclusion of a substantial concrete floor in the German design greatly adds to its strength. The stresses of shock are distributed over the whole dug-out. The roof when hit is so thick that it does not tend to bend, but is supported by the side walls. A side wall, if a shell lands near it, is supported by the roof and the floor.

The difficulties of building monolithic ferro-concrete structures in exposed positions evidently induced the enemy to employ *concrete blocks*. In fact, it may almost be said that two standard plans were used by him : monolithic concrete in rear lines where mixing and placing are easy, and concrete blocks for the front line where these operations are difficult. Examples of monolithic ferro-concrete in front lines are generally badly made, the concrete was put in in distinct layers, the iron was not clean, and the reinforcement often acted only as a plane of cleavage.

In the *early structures made of blocks*, plain concrete was used ; both walls and roof were *built in bond* on a solid bed of concrete 12 to 20 inches thick ; steel joists, rails and plates with concrete run between them were used to cover the chamber (*see* Figs. 4 and 10). Later the concrete blocks were reinforced, and *later again*, the *blocks were made with 1 inch diameter holes* :—two through the centre line of the block, and four half-circular holes in the long sides opposite them (*see* Plate 5). These holes were used for reinforcing rods, and as a key for cement mortar grouting. The experiments reported in Fieldwork Notes No. 29 indicate that concrete blocks merely bonded together in cement are not reliable as dug-out walls. In the type in which the perforated blocks were used, the floor was reinforced, and the roof, though supported on steel joists over the chamber as before, was monolithic concrete reinforced top and bottom. Thus only the walls were formed of blocks, indicating that roofs built of blocks had not proved satisfactory.

A dug-out of the last nature, size of concrete blocks 2 ft. 0 in. × 1 ft. 0 in. × 7 in., which probably had three direct hits, was still intact but cracked along each line of reinforcement. The concrete was fair. The inside, lined with wood, was completely shattered.

" This form of shelter is practically immune from shell fire ; 80 per cent. of these shelters examined were undamaged, although the entrances were blocked up in all cases . . . in one case a ' flying pig,' which landed alongside, turned the dug-out partly over, but left it otherwise intact."—(250th Tunnelling Company, R.E.)

The construction of monolithic roofs near the front, no doubt, led to difficulties, for a design dated 10-8-17, showing *blocks and girders bonded together in* concrete was evolved (*see* Plate 6).

The " Second Army Summary, 1st-15th June, Battle of Messines," states :—

" It was seen that in some instances structures of solid concrete had resisted our shell fire, but where concrete blocks were used in many instances the structure was knocked over in such a way as to render it useless and a trap for the occupants."

A few unreinforced concrete dug-outs were seen.

" They were so damaged that the occupants would have been crushed. Their ruins reminded one of the photographs of the concrete forts destroyed at the beginning of the war."—(12th Field Co., Australian Engineers.)

Some shelters have a permanent centering of strong curved corrugated iron sheets (elephant). These are generally large structures some distance behind the line and intended to shelter supports and reserves. They have a considerable thickness of concrete, 7 ft., over them. (*See* Plate 7.)

Observation posts were sometimes constructed of reinforced concrete round a built up steel plate cylinder or curved enclosure. (*See* Plate 8.) One of these had a direct hit in front which shattered the concrete, but did not damage the steel plates. The latest pattern O.P., similar to those found in the Hindenburg line, had two skins of built up 30 mm. (1·18 inch) steel plates, with 100 mm. (3·9 inches) of concrete between them. For an earlier type of O.P. *see* Plate 9.

The *machine gun emplacements* noticed were either of an early type, with thin walls ; these have been wrecked ; or they were of reinforced concrete carefully hidden inside houses or brick structures designed to imitate houses ; concealment assisted to afford these safety. No upstanding concrete emplacements could survive. The enemy has now adapted the system of keeping the M.G. crews and the guns under shelter till they are required, when they fire over the parapet. (*See* Plates 10 and 11.)

It will be noticed that Figs. 2 and 10 show a dug-out which is organised as a small defensible post with periscope or direct observation and firing step. There are various types of these. Some of them have the ceiling supported on corrugated iron arches, some on girders,

2

174

others have simply ferro-concrete roofs. In some the fire step is a plank, in others it is part of the concrete structure. This idea has been further developed in the Mebu (Mannschafts-Eisen-Beton-Unterstand) of the Hindenburg line, which has two dug-outs, two protected observation posts, a fire step for riflemen, and two niches for machine guns.

The work on Messines Ridge may be classed throughout as of fairly high standard. Most elaborate drawings of three shelters, showing the arrangement of the reinforcement and blocks in each layer, have been captured, and these indicate the care taken in construction.

The best quality concrete has probably about 8 parts of aggregate to 2 parts of matrix; the poorer class of concrete may be as weak as 8 to 1.

The aggregate is composed of water-worn gravel of flintstone and quartz (in the better class of work this gravel has been broken to about ½-in. gauge); the sand is for the most part coarse, sharp and clean. The matrix is of a good quality cement.

Bad quality concrete was also due apparently :—

    (a) To bad cement—in some cases quite dead.

    (b) To disintegrated granite having been used in the aggregate.

It is probable with British Portland cement and sand and gravel aggregate, the thickness of concrete could be considerably reduced for equal strength.

The following information as regards reinforcement has been obtained from the examination of a partly constructed reinforced concrete dug-out.

The reinforcing bars are of three sizes corresponding to our ¾-in., ½-in. and ⅜-in. round steel bars. The ¾-in. diameter bar is the one in general use.

Great care seems to have been exercised in the fixing of the reinforcement; the vertical and horizontal bars are well wired together wherever they cross.

There is ample length of bar for the purpose of locking the ends securely in the concrete.

The reinforcement in the front and back of the end wall is particularly heavy, the bars (¾-in. diameter) forming 3-in. squares.

In the side walls the vertical bars in the later types are 3-in. pitch and the horizontal 6 in. and 12 in. Horizontal stirrups are used for the purpose of holding the inside and outside bars of a wall from splaying outwards during construction.

The earlier types of shelter are not ventilated, but in the later patterns one or more vents are always introduced into the roof. All the dug-outs appear to have had stoves for heating and several have special flue holes in the back wall for the stove pipes.

Openings have also been introduced into the trench walls to serve as windows. In every case the shelters were fitted with gas and bomb-proof doors. The earlier types have wooden doors only. The later types have these doors covered with steel plate. Other recesses are introduced for storing ammunition and bombs.

Practically all the dug-outs are on trench tramways. The carrying, but for this, would be prohibitive.

Whether men can remain fit to fight or even alive in these shell-proof concrete shelters under repeated concussion still remains to be definitely determined. The evidence at present is insufficient, although it tends to show that they cannot.

"In some cases dead were found inside dug-outs which had been hit twice by 8 in. shells, but not penetrated. They may have been killed by concussion."

(105th Field Company, R.E.)

"The results of our bombardment prove that it is impossible for a human being to live in any of these dug-outs when subjected to concentrated heavy calibre artillery fire. Even in cases where the dug-outs are still practically intact in the village of Messines, the wood linings inside are shattered into many pieces showing that the concussion must have been terrific. I am satisfied that these linings are far too badly shattered for the damage to have been done by bombs thrown into the dug-outs, although of course the interior of some of the dug-outs has been injured by bombs."

(4th Australian Pioneer Battalion.)

The experience at Verdun was that the concussion due to the impact and bursting of heavy shells is severely felt by the defenders even in deep subterranean galleries.

It is suggested that the success of the Messines structures in resisting repeated direct hits disposes of any arguments in favour of *air space* as a means of stopping heavy shells; the false or outer roof would have been useless after the first hit and the inner roof after the second, unless the former were of full thickness. In this case no material would be saved by the use of air space. No air space was used by the Germans, but it would seem that a light inner chamber, say of six inch concrete, with six inch air space, inside the monoliths, might save the inmates from the effects of concussion.

The *thickness of ferro-concrete* which successfully resisted continued bombardment was from 3 ft. 6 in. to 5 ft., unless supported by a corrugated arch, when it was generally, but not always, more. (See Plate 7.)

Details of 84 structures are given in an Appendix. Practically all those that failed were early types with roofs and walls only 1 ft. to 2 ft. thick.

The majority of the shells fired at the structures at Messines were (*see* Appendix) 9·2 in., 8 in. and 6 in. howitzer.

3

At Verdun the Germans employed large numbers of 11 in., 12 in., 14·9 in., 16·5 in. (Fort Douaumont received sixty hits from 16·5 in. in 1916; Fort Moulainville 830 from 16·5 in., besides 4,940 of other calibres, February–July, 1916). The conclusions arrived at by the **French Engineer** officer who reported on the subject, were (*a*) that plain concrete is superior **to** reinforced (although he admits that a layer of metal just inside the ceiling prevented fragments of concrete from falling into the casemates); (*b*) that resistance depends greatly on the mass **of** the concrete; (*c*) that a bursting course, a layer of sand 3¼ to 5 ft. thick and a plain concrete roof, which whatever the span, must not be less than 6½ ft. thick, will resist continuous bombardment by the heaviest projectiles. Air space is not referred to in the French report.

Until further data can be obtained, the French experience and the German practice, as observed on Messines ridge, can only be reconciled by assuming that ferro-concrete 3 ft. 6 in. to 5 ft. thick, reinforced near the inner and outer surfaces, will resist the ordinary concentrated bombardment that precedes an attack, but that at least 6½ ft. of plain concrete (possibly this thickness could be reduced by use of surface reinforcement) with an elastic layer and good bursting course over it are required to withstand an intensive bombardment extending over a long period of weeks in the attack on a fortress. To obviate the effects of concussion on the occupants of a casemate, it may be advisable to provide an inner chamber.

APPENDIX.

Record of concrete structures at La Petite Douve Farm, between the farm and Messines, and on west side of Messines. (Lieut. P. B. Hudson, 4th Australian Pioneer Battalion.)

To shorten description the structures are classified under the following types:—

Type 1. Concrete with uniform reinforcement of rods, *vide* Plate 1.
Type 2. Concrete with heavy surface reinforcement, *vide* Plate 2.
Type 3. Concrete blocks, *vide* Plate 4.
Type 4. Walls of concrete block, roof of reinforced concrete, *vide* Plate 5.
Type 5. Early types with rail reinforcement.

The village of Messines and the ground on the west and south sides (Squares O·32 (c and d) and U·2 (a and b), in which the concrete structures Nos. 11 to 34 in the table below were situated, were fired on by the guns shown below. In the concentrated bombardment of Messines the average number of rounds per gun was as shown in the third column.

Number.	Guns.	Rounds per gun.
1	15-in. how.	10
8	12-in. ,,	15
48	9·2-in. how.	25
37	8-in. how.	80
96	6-in. ,,	80

What guns were firing on La Petite Douve Farm is not known exactly, but probably all natures up to 12-in. howitzers.

Although there were numerous direct hits, the number of structures wrecked or seriously damaged was only nine. Six of these, Nos. 2, 12, 14, 18, 26 and 28, had roofs and walls only 1 ft. to 2 ft. thick; the seventh, No. 31, had a roof 3 ft. thick; the two others, Nos. 3 and 8, are not described in detail, but were of an early type with rails in the reinforcement.

I.—Near La Petite Douve Farm.

No. 1. Dug-out, *Type No. 4*. Has probably had three direct hits. Still intact but has cracked along each line of reinforcement. Concrete fair. Size of concrete blocks, 2 ft. 0 in. × 1 ft. 0 in. × 7 in. Inside was lined with wood now completely shattered.

*No. 2. A machine gun emplacement in form of a decagon. *Type No. 2*. Completely blown down and shattered.

*No. 3. Dug-out, *Type No. 5*. Was completely wrecked. Roof concrete reinforced with half rails set in concrete with rods over, and three rows of 6 in. diameter wood logs over.

No. 4. Dug-out, *Type No. 3*. Wood lined and still intact. Internal dimensions 12 ft. 0 in. × 9 ft. 6 in.

No. 5. Funk hole, *Type No. 4*. 4 ft. 6 in. × 4 ft. 3 in. internal dimensions, 2 ft. 6 in. high, wall 2 ft. 0 in. thick. Roof shows use of material handy to job.

No. 6. Machine gun emplacement, *Type No. 2*. Walls 2 ft. 0 in. thick. In good order.

No. 7. Dug-out, *Type No. 2*, except that troughing is used to support ceiling, and there are two layers of logs 6 in. diameter on top of the concrete under the 13 in. earth covering.
Roof concrete 4 ft. 0 in. thick, front wall 4 ft. 5 in., side walls 3 ft. 9 in., back wall 3 ft. 0 in. Internal dimensions 7 ft. 10 in. × 10 ft. 10 in. × 4 ft. 0 in.

*No. 8. Dug-out, *Type No. 5*. Reinforcement of steel joists and 16 lb. rails. Wrecked.

No. 9. Double dug-out, each chamber 7 ft. 0 in. × 7 ft. 0 in., apparently *Type No. 5*. Concrete blocks not used, walls and roof of monolithic concrete, reinforcement to ceiling 5½ in. × 2½ in. R.S.J.

No. 10. Same type as No. 9. One direct hit on roof exposed concrete 2 ft. 0 in. deep.

II.—Between La Petite Douve Farm and Messines.

No. 11. Dug-out, *Type No. 2*, single chamber, arranged as defensive post with two holes in roof, fire step in back. Internal measurement 10 ft. 0 in. × 8 ft. 2 in. Curved ceiling of No. 12 gauge corrugated iron. Thickness arch 2 ft. 6 in. Walls 3 ft. 6 in., floor 1 ft. 6 in.

*No. 12. The remains of a concrete reinforced machine gun emplacement, *Type No. 1*. Shows a structure with walls and roof 2 ft. 0 in. thick reinforced with ½ in. and ¾ in. rods; completely shattered by direct hits.

No. 13. Dug-out similar type to No. 11 but double. Two direct hits but little damage done.

*No. 14. M.G. Emplacement, *Type No. 5*, reinforcement of 60 lb. rails and ¾ in. rods. Roof 2 ft. 0 in. thick completely shattered by two hits. Rail stanchions 60 lb. rails.

III.—West Side of Messines.

No. 15. Same Type as No. 11.

No. 16. Double dug-out, *Type No. 3*. Front wall and roof 3 ft. 6 in., side walls 3 ft. Internal dimensions of each chamber 7 ft. by 7 ft. and 3 ft. 3 in. high. Probably only steel 5½ in. by 3 in. R.S.J.s to ceiling. Signs of two direct hits, but has only shattered the concrete for 2 ft. deep.

5

No. 17.   Double dug-out similar type to No. 16. Two direct hits. Badly shaken but not wrecked. Water inside this dug-out.

No. 18.   Machine gun emplacement. *Type No. 5.* Walls and roof 1 ft. 3 in. to 1 ft. 6 in. thick. This structure has been wrecked by a direct hit in the front corner facing our old trenches.

No. 19.   Dug-out, *Type No. 2,* except that the outer layer of reinforcement is steel troughing (*see* Plate 8). Very strong. Roof 4 ft. 6 in. thick, exposed side walls 5 ft. 6 in. Shows signs of many direct hits, the reinforcement showing in places. Although hit, the inside lining is still intact. The concrete is very hard and of good quality. This dug-out appears to be shell proof to a few direct hits.

No. 20.   Dug-out similar to No. 19 ; two direct hits but still intact.

No. 21.   Observation Post (*see* Plate 8), *Type No. 2.* Built round a built-up steel-plated curved inclosure of channel iron, etc., all rivetted together and with hollows as shown. The hole in the roof just allows a man's head to go through and observe by means of the O.P. opening. One direct hit in front shattered the concrete to the steel plates but did not damage the steel plates.

No. 22.   Dug-out and O.P. (*see* Plate 9). The O.P. is reinforced concrete, apparently of *Type No. 1,* but the dug-out although concrete is not reinforced. One shell (apparently a "dud") has penetrated right through the roof into the dug-out. This structure was apparently built in a hay-stack. The concrete is good but coarse.

No. 23.   Dug-out similar to No. 16, with an annexe added later. The annexe is of reinforced concrete with rods to roof and is completely shattered.

No. 24.   Old house strengthened in inside with concrete blocks. The roof is of 60-lb. rails laid side by side.

No. 25.   Elaborate double dug-out with chambers 12 ft. 6 in. by 10 ft. 5 in. Walls of reinforced concrete up to 5 ft. thick, apparently *Type No. 2.* The brick building over this dug-out is quite wrecked, but the dug-out itself is unharmed. The walls inside are wood lined and tapestry cloth covering panelled out. It is well furnished.

No. 26.   O.P. built of cement concrete blocks, *Type No. 3 ;* walls 2 ft. thick almost completely shattered.

No. 27.   Double dug-out built in the cellar of a building. Chambers 11 ft. 6 in. by 11 ft. 6 in. and 7 ft. by 10 ft.; walls 2 ft. 5 in. thick. The old ceiling of rolled steel joists and brick ring arches still showing and intact. It, however, had been covered over with 2 ft. of concrete. The brick house is completely wrecked.

No. 28.   O.P. and Dug-out combined. The back wall was of brick only but the front and side walls were of reinforced concrete. The O.P. is of *Type No. 1.* A shell has pierced right through one wall of this construction. The wall was 12 ins. thick with a 2 ft. by 2 ft. pier alongside.

No. 29.   Next to No. 27 and of similar construction, with 4 ft. 6 in. of reinforced concrete to roof. Has several chambers and is still intact.

No. 30.   Dug-out and defensible post similar to No. 11, *Type No. 2.* Hit many times but not completely wrecked, inside wood lining shattered.

No. 31.   Small reinforced dug-out of *Type No. 1.* Roof 3 ft. thick. Blown to pieces.

No. 32.   A gun emplacement of great strength, measures 14 ft. by 10 ft. Walls and roof *Type No. 2.* Roof 4 ft. 6 in. thick. Hit over and over again. Concrete stripped on ceiling showing 3 layers of ¾ in. rods at 2 in. C. to C. Rods hit in many places but the structure still stands. A wrecked gun lies inside.

No. 33.   Dug-out and defensible post similar to No. 11, *Type No. 2.* Wall facing our old trenches blown in but structure not completely shattered.

No. 34.   Large O.P. built inside an old brick building ; brick walls blown down but O.P. not destroyed. Of great strength, roof of reinforced concrete about 4 ft. thick reinforced with steel rails, rods, etc. Measures about 15 ft. by 15 ft. on outside.

ARMY PRINTING AND STATIONERY SERVICES A—7/17—S1217—1,000.

DUGOUT WITH OBSERVATION POST

REINFORCED CONCRETE - EARLY TYPE WITH UNIFORM ROD REINFORCEMENT

From the Official Manual STELLUNGSBAU, 2nd Edition, 15 Dec. 1916

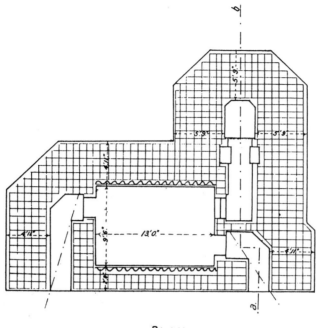

__PLAN__

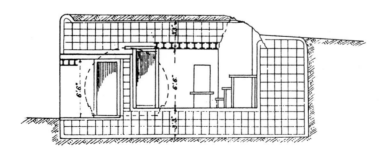

SECTION A.B.

Drawn by F.G. Newcomb, 2nd Cpl. R.E.

PRINTED BY Nº 6 ADVANCED SECTION, A.P.&S.S.

Dugout
Reinforced Concrete
Latest Pattern of Reinforcement.
Not affected by hits lower than second row of reinforcement.

9ᵀᴴ Field Cº Australian Engineers. June 1917.

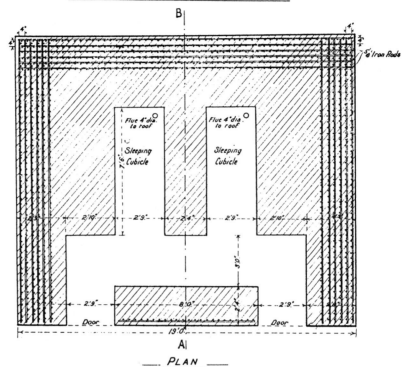

B

Flue 4"dia. to roof

Sleeping Cubicle

Flue 4"dia. to roof

Sleeping Cubicle

7'6"

⅝" Iron Rods

2'8"   2'10"   2'9"   2'4"   2'9"   2'10"   2'4"

3'0"

2'9"   8'0"   2'9"

Door   Door

19'0"

A

— PLAN —

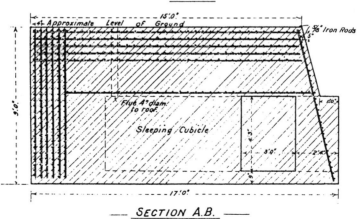

15'0"

Approximate Level of Ground

⅝" Iron Rods

Flue 4"diam. to roof

Sleeping Cubicle

3'0"

2'4"

9'0"

5'0"

17'0"

— SECTION A.B. —

PRINTED BY Nº 6 ADVANCED SECTION, A.P. & S.S.

Drawn by F.G. Newcomb,
2ᴺᵈ Cpl, R.E.

180

DUGOUT
REINFORCED CONCRETE.

This dugout shows many signs of direct hits, the reinforcement appearing in places, but the inside lining is intact.

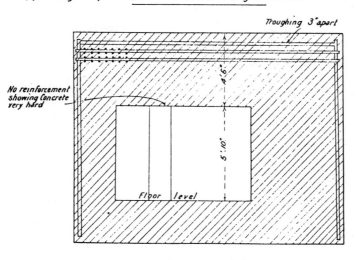

Troughing 3" apart

No reinforcement showing Concrete very hard

4'.6"

5'.0"

Floor level

SECTION A.B.

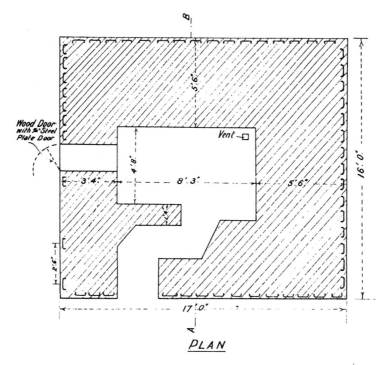

B

5'.6"

Wood Door with ⅜" Steel Plate Door

Vent

4'.8"

3'.4"   8'.3"   5'.6"

16'.0"

2'.6"

17'.0"

A

PLAN

Drawn by F.G.Newcomb
2ⁿᵈ C⁄ R.E.

DUGOUT WITH SNIPER'S POST OR LOOK OUT AND FIRE STEP.

This is standard design and specimens are found at regular intervals along the front north of St IVES.
The Concrete is heavily reinforced, especially near the surfaces, where ¹³/₁₆ U shaped round iron is used;
vertical bars are ⁷/₁₆". In the interior of the concrete ⁵/₈" bars were used.
One of the shelters examined had been hit apparently by a medium Trench Mortar, which had not broken through.

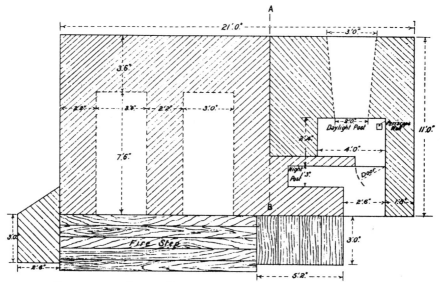

HORIZONTAL PLANE SECTION JUST ABOVE FIRESTEP

NOTE: Some shelters have no Sniper's Post and are finished off at A.B.

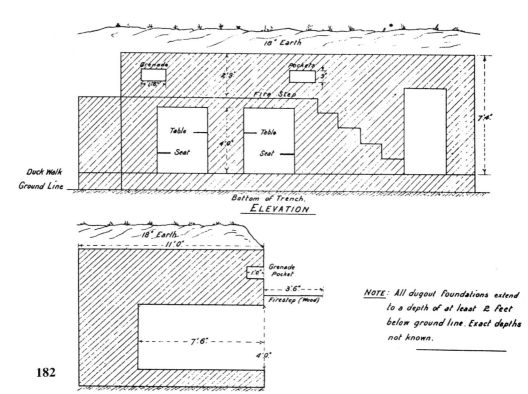

ELEVATION

NOTE: All dugout foundations extend
to a depth of at least 2 feet
below ground line. Exact depths
not known.

182

CROSS SECTION THROUGH GRENADE POCKET AND SHELTER.

Drawn by F.G.Newcomb,
2ᴺᴰ C/, R.E.

DUGOUT

CONCRETE BLOCKS AND RAILS, EARLY TYPE.

From Drawings captured at MESSINES, by 171st Coy R.E. dated March 1916.
The complete set consisted of 10 drawings.

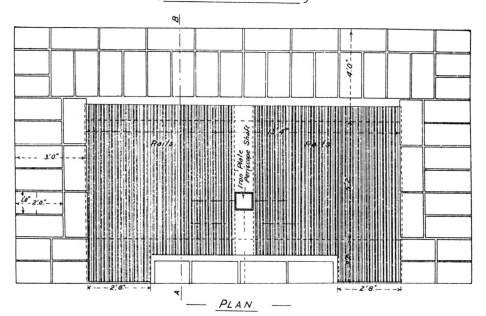

PLAN.

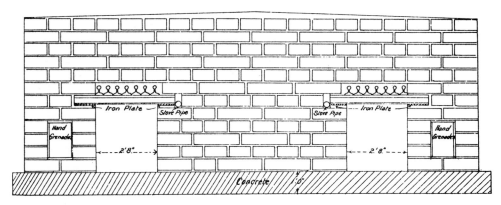

REAR ELEVATION

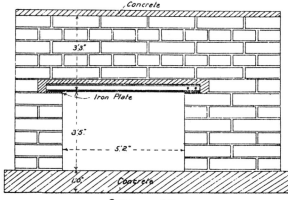

SECTION A.B.

Drawn by E.G. Newcomb
2nd Lt. R.E.

183

DUGOUT

CONCRETE BLOCK WALLS AND REINFORCED ROOF

ARRANGED AS DEFENSIBLE POST.

From Drawings found in MESSINES 17.6.17. by 12th FIELD Co AUSTRALIAN ENGRS.

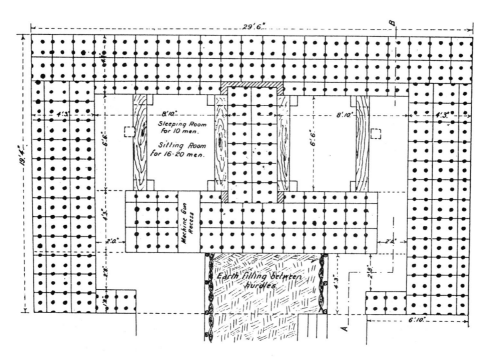

PLAN (OF FIRST LAYER)

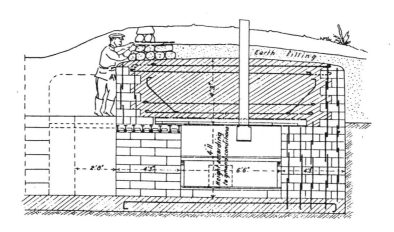

CROSS SECTION A.B.

Drawn by F.G.Newcomb,
Lt. Col. R.E.

EMERGENCY DUGOUT

OF CONCRETE BLOCKS AND STEEL JOISTS

From captured German Plan dated 10.3.17.

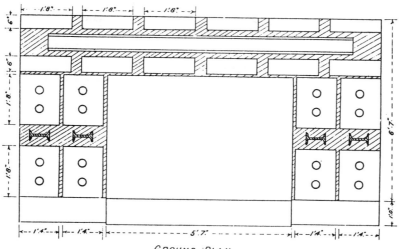

GROUND PLAN.

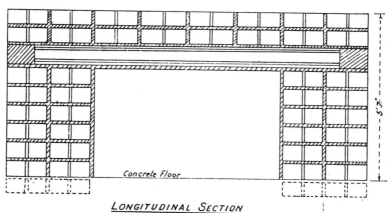

Concrete Floor

LONGITUDINAL SECTION

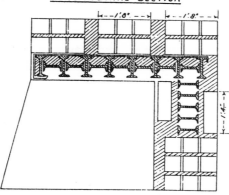

CROSS SECTION

Drawn by F.G.Newcomb,
2ᵈ Opl. R.E.

PRINTED BY N° 6 ADVANCED SECTION, A.P. & S.S.

REINFORCED CONCRETE AND ELEPHANT SECTION SYSTEM.

IN OOSTTAVERNE WOOD

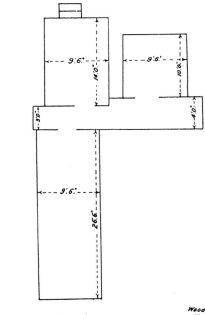

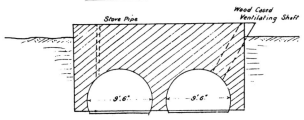

Stove Pipe

Wood Cased Ventilating Shaft

SECTION

EAST OF WYTSCHAETE

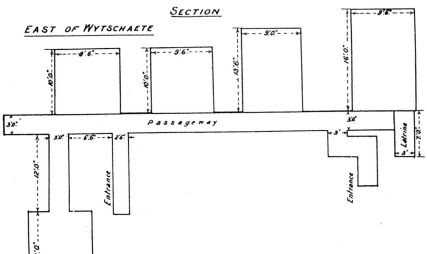

186

OBSERVATION POST

REINFORCED CONCRETE

Has two direct hits but is still intact.

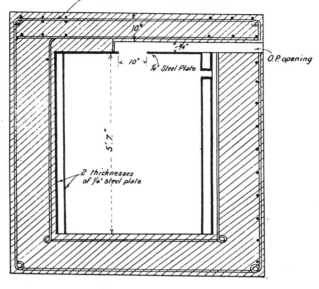

Reinforcement ¼" to ¾" Rods.
at 8" c. to c. interlaced and wired

10"

10"

¾"

¼" Steel Plate

O.P. opening

5'.7"

2 thicknesses
of ¼" steel plate

SECTION A.B.

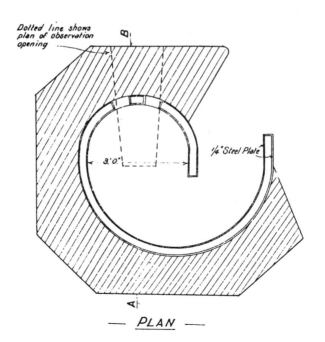

Dotted line shows
plan of observation
opening

B

¼" Steel Plate

3'. 0."

A

— PLAN —

Drawn by F. G. Newcomb
2ⁿᵈ Cpl., R.E.

PRINTED BY Nº 6 ADVANCED SECTION, A.P. & S.S.

OBSERVATION POST (IN HAY STACK)

The O.P. is of Reinforced Concrete but the Dugout is of plain Concrete.
A shell (apparently a "dud") penetrated right through the roof into the dugout.

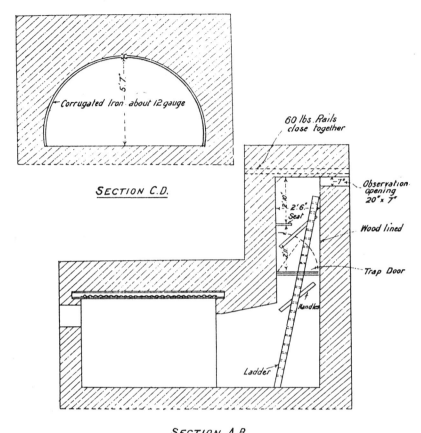

← Corrugated Iron about 12 gauge

5'-7"

SECTION C.D.

60 lbs. Rails
close together

Observation
opening
20" × 7"

7"

2'-10"

2'6".
Seat

2'-6"

Wood lined

Trap Door

Handles

Ladder

SECTION A.B.

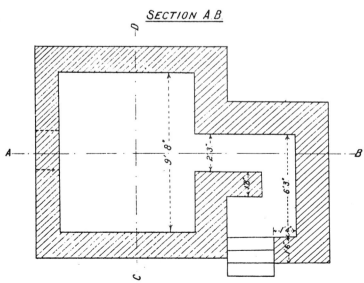

D

A ————————— B

9'-8"

2'-3"

1'8"

6'-3"

1'-4"

1'6"

C

188

PLAN.

Drawn by F.G. Newcomb,
2nd Cpl., R.E.

Dugout
on Messines Ridge

WALLS BUILT OF CONCRETE BLOCKS, REINFORCEMENT OF RAILS & CHANNELS.
This Structure was wrecked, apparently by Heavy Trench Mortar fire. Two bombs
appear to have landed near the corner and penetrated below the foundation.

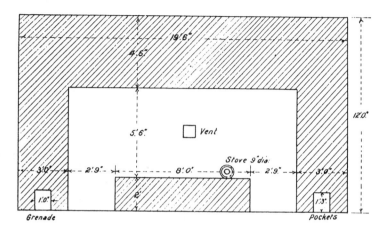

GROUND PLAN

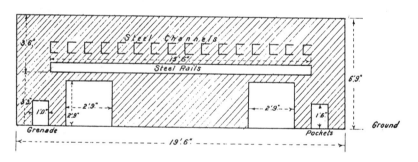

FRONT ELEVATION

NOTE: All dugout foundations extend to a depth of at least 2 feet below ground line.
Exact depths not known.

Drawn by F.G. Newcomb.
2nd Cpl. R.E.

APPENDIX II

E. in C. Fieldwork
Notes No. 43.

GERMAN CONCRETE STRUCTURES IN THE AREA NORTH OF YPRES, CAPTURED IN AUGUST, 1917, AND THE EFFECT OF SHELL FIRE ON THEM. *

(From Reports of some of the Chief Engineers, C.R.E.s. and Field Company Commanders Concerned.)

(1) The general conclusions drawn from the reports on the concrete structures on Messines Ridge, circulated in Field Works Notes No. 31, appear to be confirmed by the examination of the area north of Ypres. The classes of shelter are much the same in both localities. The only new feature observed is the tendency to divide up large shelters by substantial concrete partitions. Owing to the situation of some of the dug-outs near Ypres, a detailed examination of some of the most interesting ones has not yet been possible.

(2) There seems no doubt that the monolithic system of concrete construction with surface reinforcement continued right round and through the floor renders the structures very resisting to shell fire.

The reports state :—

　　(a) "Most of the dug-outs have been hit, and except for some in front line, where the concrete appears to have been poor, or the thickness insufficient, they have not suffered. One farm has been incessantly bombarded by ourselves and by the enemy for over a month and is none the worse."

　　(b) "Numerous structures show no sign of being damaged."

　　(c) "The effect of shell fire on these structures has been practically nil, though the surrounding ground is a mass of interlocking shell holes."

(3). Some structures were actually moved bodily without being broken up. In one case "a large shell landed on the ground close to one wall and the shelter settled down in the shell hole."

In another the shelter "was knocked slightly out of plumb without in any way cracking it."

It is also noticed that "concrete structures originally inside buildings have suffered far less damage than the others; the great value of an air space and burster is very well exemplified by this; they also render concussion inside much less."

(4) As regards the *penetration of shells into concrete reinforced with rods*, the reports say:—

　　(a) "In no case has the concrete been affected deeper than nine inches. Only two rows of reinforcement are therefore exposed to view, but it is probable that more exist."

　　(b) "The iron rod reinforcement in walls and roofs where concrete has been broken away by shell fire was practically undamaged."

　　(c) "There are numerous cases of hits which have been arrested at a layer of reinforcing bars. Sometimes the bars themselves are only broken by direct contact with the shell or pieces of shell, whereas the concrete is cracked by shock alone.

　　"In one case a shell has penetrated a wall about 1-ft. 10-ins. thick, reinforced 3-ins. from the outside surface by vertical bars $1\frac{3}{8}$-ins. diameter at a pitch of 8-ins. Only one bar is broken, but the remainder have been pushed outwards by the passage of the shell.

　　"In another wall there are two horizontal layers of steel bars about $\frac{1}{2}$-in. diameter. They are projections from the lower reinforcing of the roof of the shelter. A hit on the wall has broken off the concrete to a depth of about 2-ft. 6-ins., whereas only about three of the bars are cut, the remainder projecting from the concrete, bent but whole."

(5) As noticed at Messines, rails and joists in the mass of the concrete have an undoubted disintegrating effect. †

In many cases, especially with reinforcement of rails or heavy bars, shearing and cracking has taken place along the plane of the reinforcement when the structure has been hit, and this would appear to be a good reason for dispensing with metal except near the surfaces.

(6) The *block system of construction* is again condemned. ‡

　　(a) "All dug-outs built of concrete blocks that were hit were done in."

　　(b) "The wall of a shelter built of concrete blocks 2-ft. × 1-ft. × 7-in. pointed with mortar, but without dowelling or reinforcing, has been blown in. Practically all joints have started and the weakness of the structure is evident."

　　(c) "Both monolithic and block ferro concrete is to be seen. The blocks, however, seem mostly to have been used only for facing work."

---

　* This should be read in continuation of Field Work Notes No. 31 where details of construction will be found.

　† This is confirmed by some recent Belgian experiments, a summary of which will be issued, from which it appears that concrete reinforced throughout by a grill of bars is more quickly damaged by shell fire than concrete reinforced near the under surface only.

　‡ A recently captured document issued by the Hd. Qrs. Ypres Group 21/2/17, says :—"The thickness of walls of reinforced concrete emplacements should be at least 1.50 metres (4-ft. 11-ins). Only concrete prepared in the correct way resists bombardment. Concrete blocks do not."

(7) A new method of using blocks was found in the enemy dug-outs on the Sterling Castle Ridge (*see* sketch).   These dug-outs were formed of an " elephant " shelter 14-ft. × 9-ft. × 6-ft. high erected on a concrete floor 1-ft. thick.

The end walls were built of concrete 2-ft. thick, with door openings 2-ft. × 5-ft. ; the arch forming the side walls and roof was covered with 15-in. concrete, with an outer layer of 2-ft. concrete blocks set on end and laid in strong cement mortar.   No reinforcement is visible.

A 1-ft. partition wall of concrete in the centre of the dug-out divides it into two compartments 6-ft. 6-in. × 9-ft. 6-in.

Along the side of the dug-out facing our lines there is a protective wall 32-in. to 36-in. thick, built of concrete blocks laid in cement.

Three sizes of blocks are used of a uniform thickness of 6-in., viz. :—2-ft. × 1-ft., 16-in. × 20-in. with two grooves in each end, and 16-in. × 10-in. with one groove in each end.

" One of these dug-outs received a direct hit from a 4·2 or 5·9 which has displaced a few of the roof blocks.   It is doubtful whether they could stand a heavy crump."

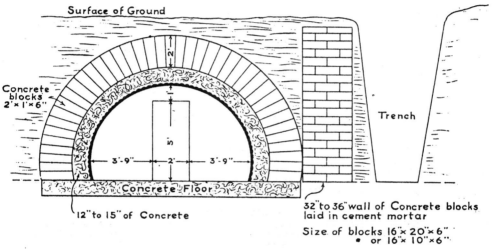

(8) The reports as to the *effects of concussion* are still at variance :—

(*a*) " I do not think there can be real protection in the small single cell type, as in several I have seen a couple of dead men apparently with no wounds on them, probably killed by concussion, and captured German orders state that they have not been found to afford protection."

(*b*) " There has been no sign in any of anyone suffering from concussion, and the enemy have occupied these dug-outs and others behind continually during bombardment with heavies, so that the presumption is the risk, if any, is not a large one."

(*c*) " In my opinion, the small low cramped type of dug-out can only serve to keep machine guns, etc., safe in ; I do not think it is possible as a rule for men to live through a heavy bombardment in them.   Where there has been a *heavy* direct hit and they are not wrecked, wood lining has been splintered."

(9) Very few *covered emplacements for machine guns* have been seen.

(*a*) " It is very noticeable that very few concrete structures contain M.G. emplacements ; the gun seems to be brought out and fired over the top."

(*b*) " I have neither seen nor heard of any structures in the old front line system which have loopholes in them.   The M.G. must have been used over the parapet."

ARMY PRINTING AND STATIONERY SERVICES A—9/17—4755S—1,000

APPENDIX III

E. in C. Fieldwork
Notes No. 48.
(This takes the place of Fieldwork Notes No. 48 (provisional), which is hereby cancelled.)

USE OF FERRO-CONCRETE IN DUG-OUT CONSTRUCTION.

INTRODUCTORY.

In the construction of dug-outs, M.G. positions, O.P.s, etc., concealment from observation by the enemy and protection from his fire are the two objects to be attained. Usually the two are materially antagonistic.

In the case of O.P.s, certain M.G. positions, etc., concealment is of primary importance. However proof an O.P. may be, it cannot be used if it is struck at frequent intervals by heavy shell; further, it must be remembered that an observation slit or M.G. embrasure may be blocked hopelessly with earth thrown up by an exploding shell. In such cases, therefore, full protection must often be sacrificed to concealment, and medium or splinter-proof cover accepted.

In the case of dug-outs for garrisons, however, full protection is the first consideration, and should be provided even at the loss of perfect concealment.

The work involved in the construction of concrete dug-outs is so great in proportion to the accommodation provided that, as a general rule, they should not be attempted, at any rate in any number, where carrying parties have to be employed, and wherever they are constructed most careful organization of the work is required if they are to be completed in a reasonable time.

The fact that the concrete takes so long to set requires that every effort should be made to have rapidity of construction. Requirements for this are :—

    1. Preparation of reinforcement to be carried out at the workshops so as to have the minimum of work on it in the field (*i.e.*, cutting to lengths and bending).

    2. Tramway facilities for delivering the materials.

    3. Continuity of supervision, both by Officers and Foremen.

    4. The unskilled labour to be changed as seldom as possible.

SOLID CONCRETE.

The comparative " shell-proof " strength of solid concrete, as compared with reinforced concrete, is shown in Appendix, para. III. *b.*

It will be seen that a great saving in weight of material used, and consequently in labour and transport, can be attained by the use of reinforcement.

FERRO-CONCRETE.

1. The value of ferro-concrete in the construction of dug-outs has been clearly proved, but unless the principles governing its use in engineering structures are followed, much valuable material will be wasted on dug-outs which are in no way stronger, and in many cases are actually weaker, than those constructed of plain concrete.

The following notes compiled from the results of experience of shell fire on dug-outs and pill boxes, and of experiments carried out, are issued for the guidance of R.E. units engaged on work of this nature.

2. While reinforcement near the surface of concrete may have the effect of checking the penetration of shell, its main value lies in increasing the tensile strength of the concrete to take up the stresses caused by the explosion. The reinforcement should, therefore, be arranged on the principles governing the construction of concrete beams or struts, in accordance with the nature of the stresses to be taken up.

The conditions, work having to be carried out at night, or under camouflage screening by day, scarcity of materials, want of skilled labour, etc., render it impossible in most cases to adopt the best practice, but provided that certain general rules are followed, the reinforcement will give a stronger structure, and will not be wasted.

These general rules are :—

    (i.) The ideal section of a concrete structure designed to resist shell fire is that of a box in which the solid bears a high proportion to the void.

    (ii.) Reinforcement is required—

        (*a*) On the inner surface and parallel to the surface of roofs, walls and floor respectively. This reinforcement contributes to the tensile strength of the concrete and also holds the concrete together, thus preventing large pieces from falling from the roof on to the occupants when it is struck by a shell.

        (*b*) On the outer surface. This reinforcement is necessary to resist penetration of the shell and also to distribute the stresses, due to the explosion of the shell, over the main mass of the concrete underneath.

        (*c*) Binding (*a*) and (*b*) together so as to resist shear and consequent horizontal lamination.

(iii.) The most suitable reinforcement for the above purposes is :—

(a) A grid of $\frac{1}{2}''$, $\frac{3}{4}''$, or up to $1\frac{1}{4}''$ steel bars arranged to form squares of 6″ to 10″ sides and wired together at the crossing places; joints in bars must have a lap of not less than twelve times the diameter.

This grid is placed about 3″ from the inner surface of the concrete.

(b) A similar grid placed about 3″ from the outer surface.

If material and time permit, a second grid can be placed about 6″ from the outer grid; this serves further to distribute the stresses due to the explosion of the shell.

NOTE.—Large mesh expanded metal, when available, can be used in place of these grids and is equally effective.

(c) Stirrups of hoop iron, stout iron wire or bar iron, binding the inner and outer reinforcements together, and spaced at 1′ to 2′ intervals.

(iv.) No reinforcement should be placed in the middle third (i.e., near the centre) of a concreted wall, roof or floor, as this is the zone of maximum shear, and the reinforcement will tend to form a plane of cleavage.

(v.) Screw pickets or tangles of barbed wire laid in the concrete of a roof, angle iron pickets placed vertically at intervals in a wall, or iron thrown in promiscuously, do not constitute reinforcement.

(vi.) Girders, rails and large bars buried in the concrete, so far from strengthening it, merely tend to crack and break it up if the mass is hit by a shell.

(vii.) Doorways and other openings should have reinforcement round them connected to roof, wall and floor reinforcement; the lintel being reinforced to support the roof, and the jambs reinforced for the full thickness of the wall to support the thrust of the side walls when struck by a shell.

Floors should be reinforced with a layer of XPM near the upper surface.

(viii.) To resist shells up to 8″, reinforced concrete roof and walls should be 3′ 6″ thick; the floor corresponding to this should be one foot thick. The equivalent in plain concrete to 3′ 6″ of reinforced is about five feet. (This applies to good concrete only.)

(ix.) Additional security can be given by a layer of two feet or more of earth on the concrete with a bursting or deflecting course over it; if there is no bursting course, earth merely acts as tamping to the explosion of the shell, and not more than about six inches should be put on to give concealment.

(x.) The resistance of concrete depends largely on being monolithic, but concrete blocks, if special measures are taken to secure them together by bonding, and by steel rods well grouted in, will afford good protection, but to obtain an equal degree of strength as mass concrete, great care must be exercised in construction.

In situ concrete takes so long to dry out that the advantages of using it as compared with blocks, which are matured before they are sent up, are largely discounted. (See also xv.)

(xi.) Air space is undoubtedly effective in reducing concussion, but as the outer roof " must be strong enough and thick enough to burst the shell and absorb the shock " (S.S.116, page 4), the construction of such spaces as part of the concrete structures means considerable work. If it is desired to reduce concussion, it is simpler to build an inner chamber one brick thick, with a wooden floor inside the reinforced concrete structure. The air space should not be enclosed, but the air should have access to the outside atmosphere.

If an air space is made above the main structure with a small amount of cover less than 5.9″ proof over, the upper roof will be rapidly destroyed by bombardment and is difficult to repair. It is, therefore, preferable to make a solid roof in the first place. (Neither the French nor the German Army employs air space.)

(xii.) Should there not be sufficient concrete available to make a 3′ 6″ reinforced roof, mixed cover can be substituted (See S.S. 116). Such mixed cover might consist, counting downwards, of :—

1. A few inches of earth for concealment.

2. A layer of hard stuff (stone, concrete, brickbats, etc., in sandbags), not less than one foot thick, to aid in bursting and deflecting ordinary shells.

3. A layer of earth or soft stuff, 2′ to 3′ thick, to minimise concussion.

4. Reinforced or plain concrete, not less than 1′ 6″ thick, and as much thicker as can be conveniently arranged.

(xiii.) The lower ends of walls should be carried as low as possible to prevent them being overturned by a shell bursting under them. Protecting them by an apron is also useful.

(xiv.) For all dug-out work, a strong quick-setting concrete is required of the best materials, in the proportion by volume of about one of cement to two of sand and four of broken stone. It should be well rammed, but built continuously, so as to form one mass. The aggregate used round the reinforcement should be of small stuff, $\frac{1}{2}''$—$\frac{3}{4}''$ gauge.

(xv.) Internal centering should not be removed until the concrete has well set; vibration or movement will cause separation between soft concrete and reinforcement, and seriously weaken the structures. Otherwise the concrete should be left as much as possible exposed to the air in order to accelerate the drying out, which is a long process with thick masses of concrete.

2

(xvi.) Free through ventilation is essential in all concrete dug-outs to get rid of poison gas from gas shells and to minimise concussion, which is always much greater than in mined dug-outs. Earth cushions are also valuable for reducing concussion.

Specimen designs are attached:—

Plate.

1. 8″ shell-proof cover for two machine-gun detachments.

2. 5.9″ shell-proof cover for six to eight men.

3. Machine gun emplacement where concealment will only permit of medium protection against field guns.

4. 5.9″ shell-proof cover arranged for 40 men in an existing building.

5. 5.9″ shell-proof cover (mixed cover).

6. 5.9″ shell-proof cover formed of plain concrete in a mined building.

APPENDIX (PENETRATION OF SHELL).

I. The effect of a shell striking any dug-out depends upon:—

(*a*) Its velocity, or the range from which it has been fired.

(*b*) The type of fuze used, *e.g.*, graze, percussion, or delay action. (N.B.—The Germans sometimes fire armour-piercing shell against dug-outs.)

(*c*) The angle at which the shell strikes the target. A glancing blow is much more ineffective than one at right angles.

It is due to these varying factors, which are often impossible to ascertain in practice, that such discordant results are reported.

II.* Precis of experiments on good concrete made in February-March, 1917, with 5·9″ shells, striking velocity 820 f.s.; angle of impact, a right angle for experiments 1 to 4 below.

1. Built up sandbags filled with shingle. 13 ft. thickness penetrated.

2. Two layers of logs (4″ to 6″ thick) with earth behind. Penetration into earth 10′—18′.

3. Concrete slabs, 2′ x 1′ x 4″ reinforced with iron rods. Penetration 3½′ to 4′ 9″.

4. Ditto, reinforced with expanded metal. Penetration 2′ 9″ to 3′ 10″.

5. *At ordinary angles of descent 12″ of reinforced concrete slabs was just proof.*

6. The penetration into a large monolith of plain concrete (3 ft. thick) at the *ordinary angles of descent* was never more than 4 inches, showing a marked improvement over penetration into slabs. (*Vide* 5 above.)

7. Experiments with earth cushions *between bursting courses and the concrete* led to the conclusion that 2′ 6″ should give sufficient security, as a general rule, for the roof, and not less than 3′ 3″ for the walls.

III. (*a*) The French consider that the following is the amount of cover required to resist various shells:

Shell.	Soil.	Penetration.	Cover required.
8″	1 (soft soil)	10 ft.	22 ft.
	2 (hard soil)	8 ,,	17 ,,
	3 (very hard soil or chalk)	7 ,,	15 ,,
12″	1	15 ,,	28 ,,
	2	12 ,,	23 ,,
	3	10 ,,	20 ,,

Our practice is to provide 30 ft. of cover in soil 1, 25 ft. in soil 2, and 20 ft. in soil 3. The thickness of cover required exceeds considerably the actual penetration, so that the dug-out may be protected from the effects of concussion and blast.

(*b*) The thicknesses of masonry and concrete considered proof by the French are as follows:—

Shell.	Masonry.	Concrete.	Reinforced Concrete.
8″	7 ft.	5 ft.	3¼ ft.
12″	7½ ,,	6 ,,	4 ,,
15″	8¼ ,,	7 ,,	5 ,,

(*c*) A typical concrete shelter constructed by the French consists of:—

(*a*) Casing of shelter, 1½′—1¾′ masonry.

(*b*) Centre layer, 3′—3½′ loose rubble.

(*c*) Top layer, 2½′ reinforced concrete.

* E. in C. Fieldwork Notes No. 29.

The idea is that the top layer of reinforced concrete bursts the shell, the centre layer of rubble absorbs concussion, while the inner casing preserves the shelter inside and keeps out splinters and débris. The top layer of reinforced concrete is spread several feet beyond the actual shelter.

It will be noticed that this type differs from that adopted either by us or the Germans.

Laying good concrete on the top of made earth and spoil is not easy, as it is difficult to consolidate it properly.

IV.   Effect of *minenwerfer* shell (German observations).

A.   *Full-sized heavy H.E. shell.*

      1.   Non-delay action.

Destructive effect not sufficient against deep-mined dug-outs. Against shallow dug-outs, there is an annihilating effect due to concussion.

      2.   Delay action fuze.

Very great penetration. Mined dug-outs with 23 to 30 feet of earth cover are blown in; the craters in average soil are 16 to 20 feet deep and 26 to 33 feet in diameter.

B.   *Medium H.E. shell.*

      1.   Non-delay action.

Deep dug-outs are not destroyed; they have a good effect in open trenches due to concussion.

      2.   Delay action fuze.

Mined dug-outs, 10 to 13 feet in depth, are blown in.

C.   *Light H.E. shell of all types.*

Effect at close range and high angles of elevation similar to that of a field-gun H.E. shell.

Plate 1.

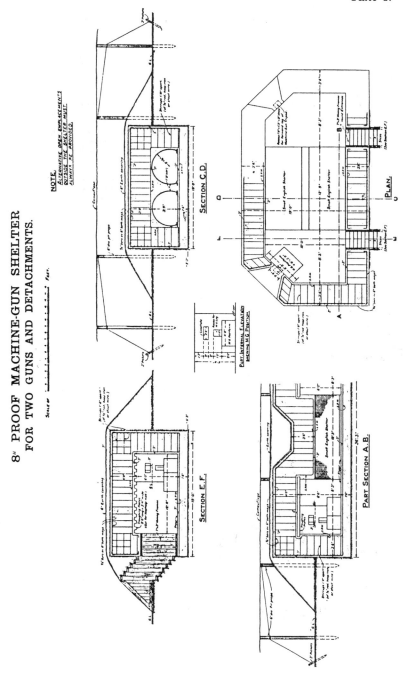

8" PROOF MACHINE-GUN SHELTER
FOR TWO GUNS AND DETACHMENTS.

5·9 PROOF REINFORCED CONCRETE SHELTER
FOR 6 TO 8 MEN.

SCALE OF |⎯⎯⎯|⎯|⎯|⎯|⎯|⎯|⎯|⎯| FEET

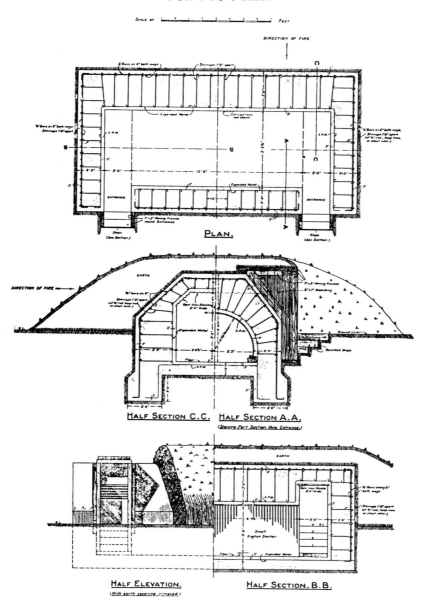

PLAN.

HALF SECTION C.C.   HALF SECTION A.A.
(Showing Part Section thro' Entrance.)

HALF ELEVATION.   HALF SECTION B.B.
(With earth covering removed.)

6

Plate 3.

MACHINE-GUN EMPLACEMENT
FOR ENFILADE FIRE WHERE CONCEALMENT IS NECESSARY, MEDIUM PROTECTION ONLY BEING POSSIBLE.

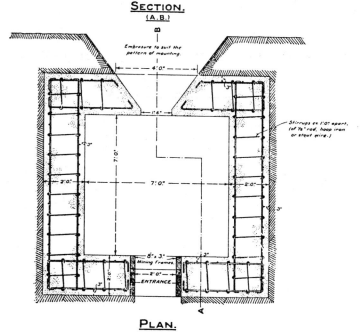

SECTION.
(A.B.)

PLAN.

Plate 4.

5·9 PROOF REINFORCED CONCRETE SHELTER
FOR 40 MEN IN EXISTING BUILDING.

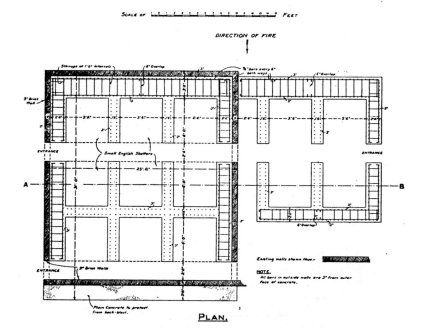

PLAN.

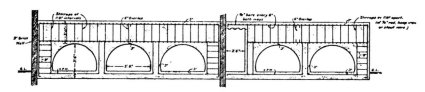

SECTION A.B.

Plate 5.

LARGE ELEPHANT SHELTER
WITH MIXED COVER.

Scale of |___|___|___|___|___|___|___|___|___|___|___| Feet

NOTE.
This may be taken to be
5' 9" shell proof.

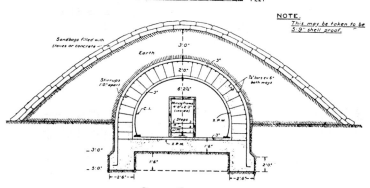

CROSS SECTION.

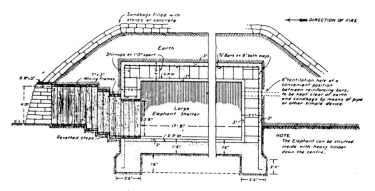

LONGITUDINAL SECTION.

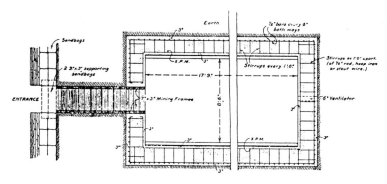

PLAN.

9

Plate 6.

CONCRETE SHELTER
IN RUINED BUILDING.

NOTE. If desirable the concrete protection can be reinforced.

SCALE OF |⊢⊢⊢⊢⊢⊢⊢⊢⊢⊢| FEET

DIRECTION OF FIRE

NOTE.
This may be taken as 3'9" shell proof with a roof 3'6" thick. when the concrete is reinforced it may be taken as 8" proof.

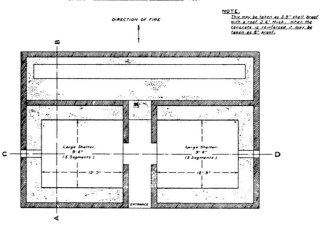

PLAN.

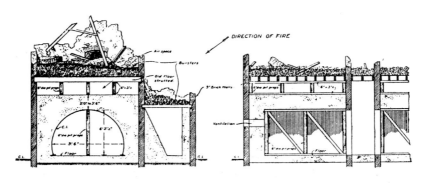

SECTION A.B.   SECTION C.D.

PRESS A—2/18—5784S—1,500.

INDEX